RETHINKING CRIMINOLOGY

Volume 27
SAGE RESEARCH PROGRESS SERIES IN CRIMINOLOGY

SAGE RESEARCH PROGRESS SERIES IN CRIMINOLOGY

Published in Cooperation with the American Society of Criminology
Series Editor: **MICHAEL R. GOTTFREDSON,** *State University of New York at Albany*
Founding Series Editor: **JAMES A. INCIARDI,** *University of Delaware*

SAGE RESEARCH PROGRESS SERIES IN CRIMINOLOGY
VOLUME 27

RETHINKING CRIMINOLOGY

edited by HAROLD E. PEPINSKY

Published in cooperation with the
AMERICAN SOCIETY of CRIMINOLOGY

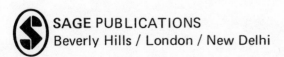 SAGE PUBLICATIONS
Beverly Hills / London / New Delhi

For information address:

SAGE Publications, Inc.
275 South Beverly Drive
Beverly Hills, California 90212

SAGE Publications India Pvt. Ltd.
C-236 Defence Colony
New Delhi 110 024, India

SAGE Publications Ltd
28 Banner Street
London EC1Y 8QE, England

Printed in the United States of America

Library of Congress Cataloging in Publication Data

Main entry under title:

Rethinking criminology.

    (Sage research progress series in criminology ; v. 27)
    "Published in cooperation with the American Society
of Criminology."
    Bibliography: p.
    1. Crime and criminals—United States—Addresses,
essays, lectures. 2. Paradigms (Social sciences)—
Addresses, essays, lectures. I. Pepinsky, Harold E.
II. American Society of Criminology. III. Title.
IV. Series.
HU6789.R415 1982   364'.973   82-10696
ISBN 0-8039-1890-9
ISBN 0-8039-1891-7 (pbk.)

FIRST PRINTiNG

CONTENTS

Harold E. Pepinsky
Indiana University

INTRODUCTION

THE CRIMINOLOGICAL MOLD

As Leslie T. Wilkins has put it, we have little knowledge about crime because criminologists are molded to "confuse the problem of crime with the problem of the criminal," to believe that something peculiar to the offender, or something in the way the offender is treated, makes or breaks crime.

Every major theory of causes of crime, including Marxist theories, assumes that people's propensity to violate the law is correlated with poverty, with the existence of what criminologists of the nineteenth century called "the dangerous classes." Within this criminological mold, rival theories rise to ascendancy, fall, and rise again. Criminologists argue over whether the primary source of the malady of the poor is genetic or traceable to some other form of eternal damnation, or in failure of nurture, nourishment, or education of the children, or in blocked aspirations, or as a normal waste product of any societal organism, or subjugation to political or economic oppression, or as a failure of help or hurt or holding of poor crooks.

The permanent ascendancy of one of the theories over others is a logical impossibility. Since the causes of crime are selected for their association with poverty as the preeminent correlate of officially known criminality, the causes—in statisticians' terms—are collinear by design. They largely relate to crime as they relate to one another. The distinct contribution of each cause is unstable, and not surprisingly appears and disappears sample by sample of criminality. In a population with a distinct group of poor offenders, the best prediction of criminality turns out to be (a) that all those who have never gotten into trouble with the law never will, and (b) that there is no known cure for a confirmed recidivist save the passage of time. As prediction is elaborated, error accumulates. We come back to the simple truth, in Reiman's (1979) terms, that as "the rich get richer and the poor get prison," a select group of increasingly dispossessed poor becomes the only group we can reliably identify as crooked, after it is too late to do anything about it (Pepinsky, 1980: 171-281).

Self-report studies and studies of white-collar crime like Reiman's can even lead one to the conclusion that the rich hurt others by breaking the law more than the poor. But the work of some criminologists, including those in this volume, suggests a more radical, more fundamental premise. Let us assume, much as Sutherland (1940) proposed more than 40 years ago, that a member of any class is no more or less likely than any other to hurt people by violating the law. Is it possible to build knowledge of crime without first isolating a class of offenders to study? If it is possible, as the work in this volume implies, then criminologists are capable of breaking the mold of confusing the problem of crime with the problem of the criminal.

Longmire's Constraints

In Chapter 1, Longmire describes constraints that governmental funding places on the study of crime. A substantial percentage of his respondents reported denial of funding for investigations of the relationship of the political economy to crime and criminal justice. His findings correspond to the experience of many of us who have known people trying to do research even in supposedly established areas like white-collar crime. We have, for instance, seen reviewers' comments that the problems to be studied were not as important as traditional issues, like whether punishment deters violent street crime.

Some observers, like Quinney (1980), have argued that a ruling class is responsible for such restrictions. The argument has some merit. Who would not rather be dissociated from the stigma and burden of being held responsible for the crime problem? If those who want someone else held responsible for crime have the money and power to dominate election and selection of officials who distribute grant funds and set crime control priorities, then the rich do restrict the growth and application of knowledge about crime.

At the same time, criminologists cannot lay all blame for restrictions on others. We lay a lot of restrictions on ourselves. A teacher can allow budding criminologists to raise issues outside the criminological mainstream, but many teachers instead grade students on how well they memorize mainstream truths. Colleagues who evaluate the work of peers for retention or promotion can give special recognition to those who struggle to articulate and pursue new questions about crime, but many do not. Journal and grant reviewers could err on the side of approving novel inquiries, but many do not. Colleagues could defy college or university administration pressure to bring in grant money by doing low-cost field and library studies, but many instead press one another to obtain grants to please the administrators. In effect, criminologists could band together to become civilly disobedient about staying within the criminological mold, but few do. As Longmire puts it: "It is to be expected that research endeavors falling outside the dominant world view of the criminological community will be difficult to generate." But why should we excuse ourselves from doing what is difficult, if we believe it is right?

Many of us in the criminological community scarcely read outside the mainstream or allow ourselves to reflect and imagine anything but convention. A primary purpose of this volume is to indicate that divergence from the mainstream is possible, to demonstrate that criminologists who fit no mold but that of their own making deserve to be published, read, rewarded, and even emulated. The first barrier to breaking the mold is in the mind of each criminologist, who has to be able to conceive of alternatives in order to try to pursue them. There are many unorthodox directions criminologists can take, as the variety of perspectives in this volume illustrates.

THE NEED TO BREAK THE MOLD

My second chapter is designed to show a need to break the criminological mold. The classical objective of any science or quest for knowledge is to gain control, if not over groups of people then at least over production of data. If a criminologist hypothesizes that crime rates will decline with an increase in punishment, the test of whether the criminologist knows anything is whether the decline in crime rates indeed follows the increase in punishment.

The trouble is that if we define "crime" as "unlawful behavior," we confront increasingly ambiguous measures of the size of or trends in the problem. When we try to prove or refine the validity of measures of crime or criminality, we fall into an infinite regress of loss of control over the theoretical significance of the measures. Today, for example, victim survey figures indicate that some crime rates are falling in the United States, while police figures indicate they are rising. The only way out of the infinite regress is to resort to tautology—the only proof of anything. On their face, our measures are indices of confinement of persons or cases. If, then, we were to redefine criminology as the study of confinement, we could gain control over our subject matter. Whether or not "confinement" becomes the phenomenon we seek to control, the need somehow to redefine the object of our inquiry is manifest.

NEW PREMISES

People are prone to divide parts of the world into two parts: good and evil, mind and body, spiritual and secular, positive and negative, normal and abnormal, to name a few. This is also known as two-value, or binary, logic. In criminology, we have all too often fallen into the two-value trap, supposing that if one criminological premise is false, a single alternative must be true, or that if the alternative is false, the original premise must be true.

Each of the three chapters in this section poses a third premise in place of a conventional distinction. Each offers a way to transcend equally unpalatable choices of how to address important criminological issues, just as Bateson's porpoises (see Chapter 2) resolved double binds.

Bohm's Myths

One of the unfortunate binds criminologists have gotten into in recent years is to assume that if one escapes the conventional mold, one must be a Marxist. Admittedly, Americans particularly need to outgrow the phobia of Marxism that has dominated political and academic life since the 1917 Russian Revolution. Our field is liberated insofar as we accept and hear Marxist colleagues, and the education offered us by forums for good Marxist scholarship, like *Crime and Social Justice,* serves us well. However, we might do well to transcend choosing between accepting the current political order, or rejecting it in favor of socialism or communism.

Bohm questions premises underlying the Marxist/non-Marxist dichotomy in criminology. "Capitalism" both imperfectly describes Western industrial orders and is not a concept Marx or Engels even used. Marx and Engels themselves never supposed that "socialism" would prevent crime, and there is no necessary relation between socialism in any form (including fascism) and crime control. It is questionable whether any political order necessarily follows that criticized by Marx and Engels, and it is more questionable that communism is practicable. Bohm concludes by suggesting some ways criminologists might "stop arguing in generalities (e.g., socialism vs. capitalism) and . . . engage in the difficult task of specifying which indicators of contemporary social formations must be changed if the problem of crime is to be resolved."

Braithwaite's Paradoxes

In Chapter 4 Braithwaite does just what Bohm asks criminologists to do, but does it in a way Bohm probably had not imagined. In the process, Braithwaite takes on another criminological premise: that the only acceptable alternative to the injustice of punishing the poor more than the rich is to treat like cases alike. He argues that one way or the other, criminal justice officials are bound to punish selectively. That being the case, criminologists can do no better than consider which form of injustice is preferable to others.

Braithwaite proposes that for the sake of both *lesser* injustice and the efficacy of crime control, we study and try ways to load selective punishment against the rich.

Marxist critics might argue that such change will not be permitted by the rich so long as they remain rich—until the poor rise up to dispossess them. They would say that we must understand and attack *the* basic cause of our problem: the survival of the ruling class. There is a logical trap here. Identifying the enemy does not imply how to undo the enemy's oppression. Even Marx went so far as to propose that in a place like the United States, class revolution might be accomplished through existing legal channels. Either "the ruling class" is invincible or it is potentially vulnerable to any number of lines of attack. If enough of us worked as Braithwaite proposes to reverse the bias of the criminal justice system, we might bring off one form of revolution.

Anderson-Sherman's Multiple Realities

While Braithwaite would have us reconceptualize justice under law, Anderson-Sherman (Chapter 5) would have us consider whether to have conflict defined as a matter of crime in the first place. A case study of the conflict between the Kikuyu and the British in Kenya leads him to conclude that the British would have been better served by negotiating cultural autonomy for the Kikuyu than by defining politically organized Kikuyu as a criminal terrorist group called "the Mau Mau." More generally, it is questionable whether much of what is defined as "terrorism" should not be treated as conflict among equals to be mediated rather than as defiance of government to be punished as crime.

There is an interesting connection between the analyses of Braithwaite and Anderson-Sherman. In the realm of repressive or restrictive social control, people who would exercise control have a basic choice of strategy: dumping up or dumping down. In fact, it is also a personal choice all of us face in day-to-day interaction as to which of two groups—those with more power than we, or peers and subordinates—to call to account for rule violation, and which to treat as potential allies through negotiation of conflict. The general human propensity is to try to negotiate with superiors and litigate against peers and subordinates, that is, to dump *down*. Together, Braithwaite and Anderson-Sherman would have us turn this propensity on its head. Braithwaite would have us litigate against superiors, and Anderson-Sherman would have us negotiate with subordinates—that is, dump *up*. This is the stuff of revolutionizing crime control in particular and social control in general. The revolutionary strategy would appear to reduce class disparities, while the conventional strategy exacerbates them. Braithwaite and Anderson-Sherman have launched a frontal attack on the mold of confusing the problem of crime with the problem of the criminal.

Harrison's Addict

Breaking a mold of thinking requires a sense of absurdity. While Bohm makes clear that conventional sense about capitalism, socialism, and crime is nonsense, while Braithwaite explicitly refers to paradoxes in thinking about biased law enforcement, while Anderson-Sherman attacks a definition of "reality," Harrison's Chapter 6 goes so far as to poke fun at the idea of prohibiting use or possession of opiates. Human beings produce their own opiates, called "endorphins," and Harrison speculates that marathon runners are more heavily addicted than many veteran mainliners of heroin. People's survival rests in part on habitual opiate production and use. By the time his analysis is finished, principled narcotics enforcement has become a contradiction in terms.

I must admit to feeling sheepish after reading Harrison's analysis. I am among those who have called upon criminologists to address higher levels of abstraction about social structure and to ignore biological sources of criminality. Just as Braithwaite perverts Marxist criminology by calling for revolution within the system, so Harrison perverts *social* science by calling for initial focus on biological processes within individuals. Harrison demonstrates that it may be practical to attack the criminological mold on the level of individual body chemistry, with an eventual impact on political and economic systems. He demonstrates that we can ill afford to reject alternatives at any level of a social system.

NEW DIRECTIONS

Some alternatives rest not on changing direction in current criminology but on filling voids in current research—areas that are largely unaddressed and that represent quantum jumps from current approaches to inquiry. Denzin's Chapter 7 is the first of such alternatives in this volume, in a section of the volume that moves from the individual to the general social structural level.

Denzin's Interpretation of Power

In Chapter 7, Denzin calls on criminologists to study how those who seize power to hurt others rationalize their behavior, to reexamine their own premises about personal use of power. It could well be that premises we share with "criminals" make crime possible, that the mold we allow to bind our thinking about how we ourselves use power contributes to the crime problem. Drawing on personal accounts to people committing crime, including Dostoyevsky's fictional account of the murderer Raskolnikov in *Crime and Punishment,* Denzin makes a persuasive case that under the right circumstances, we would probably think in the same molds as they and would be capable of raw violence.

If earlier authors have called upon us to substitute new premises about power for old, Denzin's proposal that we interpret the meaning of criminality close up offers a vehicle for becoming self-conscious about the mold that constrains our thinking about crime, a means to freeing ourselves to entertain alternative premises about crime and power. Like Harrison's, Denzin's study of the makeup of individuals becomes a vehicle for criticizing the political structure that surrounds groups of individuals. Denzin offers a profound message: If the control of crime is to lie within our power, we must accept personal responsibility for changing the way we think about dealing with others as a starting point. Otherwise, we are prisoners of our own making.

Pontell's System Capacity

In Chapter 8, Pontell outlines a new way to look at the dynamics of criminal justice. Conventionally, criminologists examine the impact of criminal sanctions on levels of crime. Pontell asks us to do the reverse: to examine the impact of levels of crime on criminal justice practices. With a focus on deterrence, Pontell discusses implications of finding that higher levels of crime impair odds, swiftness, and severity of punishment (and, one might add, increase one's odds of being punished periodically and longer). Pontell's inquiry into "system capacity" is a worthy heir to Wilkins's (1964) introduction of the systems perspective into the study of crime. Pontell draws together a wealth of literature pointing to the criminal justice system's breaking down more as we lay more "crime" on it. Somehow, we have to manage to produce less crime for the criminal justice system to handle. If the propensity of informal social control systems to feed people and cases to the criminal justice system is to be reduced, then the capacity of informal control systems to tolerate deviance must be increased. The suppression of deviance is neither desirable (Pepinsky, 1982) nor possible through repression (see Wilkins, 1964, on "deviance amplification").

Deviance—or, as psychologists call it, "deviation"—is an ambiguous term. By becoming President of the United States, one deviates from American norms of status achievement. P. Pepinsky (1961) points out that nonconformity may be accepted or deemed normal or legitimate— that is, "productive." Other nonconformity is rejected as eccentric, psychotic, parasitic, or dangerous. By contrast, seen formally, "crime" is negative conformity—a defiant recognition that one's behavior ought to be oriented by norms. Crime and disorder of the criminal justice system will increase the less likely it is that nonconformity is deemed productive, both because nonconformity is less tolerated and because resistance to pressure to conform mounts in the form of defiance. The question becomes: What interventions are more likely than others to lead nonconformity to be deemed productive? Or in Denzin's terms, how can people manage to take deviance for granted? I surmise that Friedrichs calls on us to address these questions.

Friedrichs's Crisis of Legitimacy

In the concluding chapter, Friedrich calls upon criminologists to turn from Durkheim's presumption that people need crime to help themselves stick together to a premise from Weber: "In an increasingly rationalized society, legitimation of law and the legal system becomes increasingly problematic." Friedrichs insightfully characterizes the nub of the American crime problem today as a crisis of legitimacy.

As a matter of fact, legitimacy of law and legality goes hand in hand with legitimacy of nonformity throughout a society. In one direction, it seems safe to assume that legitimacy of nonconformity implies failure to resort to criminal process. In the other, as Pontell notes, the criminal justice system appears to work better when it is used less.

P. Pepinsky (1961) has found that political sponsorship is required for nonconformity to become viewed as productive or legitimate. This finding is corroborated, for example, by Pines (1979), who found that children who transcended as unusually poor birthright had some well-connected patron. The more people there were who made the community safe for actual or potential deviants, the less crime there would be, which would imply that the criminal process was working better.

In essence, people become political sponsors for nonconformity insofar as they dump up and negotiate down—that is, insofar as they give way to subordinates' claims to protection of rights or negotiate resolution of conflict with peers and subordinates, and subject superiors to claims of right, by negotiation if possible and by resort to force—including force of law—if necessary. Friedrichs's focus on how to address the crisis in legitimacy in the United States brings this volume full circle. Longmire practically demands that funding agencies support nonconforming research by peer and subordinate criminologists. Bohm asks that we rise above, fail to conform to, the battle between conventional and Marxist criminology. I suggest criminologists will learn more about controlling crime if they can figure ways to avoid confining criminals. Braithwaite literally asks that the criminal process dump up more than down. Anderson-Sherman asks that the power of government to criminalize opposition by labeling it "terrorism" not be conceded merely because government holds a monopoly on force. Harrison uses the logic of legal right to attach governmental attempts to dictate naturally variant levels of morphine in each of our bodies. Denzin asks us to become more self-conscious about our personal exercise of power. Pontell asks us to question (or in the scientific parlance, "study") consequences of choosing protectors who have the biggest guns and prisons at their disposal. Together, the preceding chapters imply a range of approaches to Friedrichs's crisis of legitimacy, each calling for acceptance of nonconformity inside and outside criminology.

CONCLUSION

Chapter 2 argues a need for criminologists to indulge in what Bateson called "Level 3" thinking. They need to break the criminological mold and inquire from premises and in directions independent of convention.

They need to fail to conform. Which approach will gain more adherents, which will prove more effective in controlling crime as criminologists want, remains to be seen. One can only project that the greater the rate of nonconformity, the more imminent the breakthrough criminologists as a group achieve in knowing about what it takes to make crime go up or down. That breakthrough would be Bateson's "Level 4," amounting to resolution of a triple bind in human endeavor. It should be possible.

Working with the contributors to put this volume together has broadened my horizons for studying crime considerably. Heartfelt thanks go to them, Mike Gottfredson, and Sage Publications for the opportunity, and to Marsha Davis and Mary DeShong for helping prepare the manuscript. When trying to break the criminological mold, it is nice to be in such good company.

REFERENCES

PEPINSKY, H. E. (1982) "Humanizing social control." Humanity and Society (August).
———— (1980). Crime Control Strategies: An Introduction to the Study of Crime. New York: Oxford.
PEPINSKY, P. N. (1961) "The social dialectic of productive nonconformity." Merrill-Palmer Quarterly of Behavior and Development 7 (April): 127-137.
PINES, M. (1979) "Superkids." Psychology Today 12 (January): 53-63.
QUINNEY, R. (1980) Class, State, and Crime. New York: Longman.
REIMAN, J. (1979) The Rich Get Richer and the Poor Get Prison: Ideology, Class, and Criminal Justice. New York: Wiley.
SUTHERLAND, E. H. (1940) "White-Collar Criminality." American Sociological Review 5 (February): 1-12.
WILKINS, L. T. (1964) Social Deviance: Social Action, Policy, and Research. Englewood Cliffs, N.J.: Prentice-Hall.

I

THE CRIMINOLOGICAL MOLD

Dennis R. Longmire

Ohio State University

1

THE NEW CRIMINOLOGIST'S ACCESS
TO RESEARCH SUPPORT
Open Arms or Closed Doors?

The relative degree of autonomy that exists for the criminologist in selecting the substance of intellectual inquiry is the general focus of this chapter. Recently, the criminological community has been informed that the academic setting provides an air of "academic freedom" which serves to protect the autonomy of the researcher. Inciardi and Siegal (1981): 167) distinguish between the academician and the contract researcher to the effect that the university-based criminologists "exercise almost absolute control over the subject, content, and method of their work." In a similar vein, Cressey (1978) argues that the proper place for criminologists is in "ivory towers," where they can be free to pursue whatever topics they find intellectually stimulating.

To suggest that there are literally no constraints placed on the academic criminologist's inquiry by pressures other than those originating in the moral structure of the individual investigator would be naive. As Sagarin (1980a) recently argued, all sciences have areas where researchers are advised to "tread lightly." He further observes, however, that in the criminological discipline, there seems to exist more of a sensitivity to ideological points of view than to specific subject matter. The criminologist, according to this argument, is constrained more by the existing ideology than by the subject matter of a research endeavor. Taboos do

AUTHOR'S NOTE: An earlier draft of this chapter was presented at the 33rd Annual Meetings of the American Society of Criminology, Washington, D.C., November 1981.

exist restricting criminological research, but not in the sense that certain topics cannot be examined. Instead, those who choose to engage in research in certain areas are greeted with suspicion or contempt by their professional colleagues.

In several of the essays published by Sagarin (1980b) regarding the question of whether or not there should be taboos in criminology, we are informed that there are at least informal proscriptions on researchers who would examine areas such as the relationship between feminism and crime (Henson, 1980; Levin, 1980); the relationships among race, IQ, and crime (Gordon, 1980; Karmen, 1980; Levin, 1980); and the general sociobiological approach to crime (Jeffery, 1980).

Whether or not these taboos manifest themselves regarding the "new criminology" is the specific focus of this chapter. The acceptance of a Marxist criminology in the United States has been discussed by Platt (1974), and from his perspective there is good reason to believe that researchers interested in Marxist criminology will be greeted with considerable contempt from their more traditional colleagues. An excellent example of this response can be seen in Geis and Meier's (1978) finding that there was considerable consensus among criminology's leading scholars that the least healthy development in the discipline was the interjection of ideology into the study of crime. While all of these scholars were not specific, the Marxist perspective was cited as the most notable development in this regard.

In line with the logic of Kuhn (1970), it is to be expected that research endeavors falling outside the domain of the dominant world view of the criminological community will be difficult to generate. According to Kuhn's perspective, scientific growth includes several stages, one of which is the stage of "normal science" during which the dominant paradigm is subject to numerous attempts to clarify and expand on it. During this process of clarification, minor revisions are expected to be made in the general theories being posited or in the methodologies in popular use; however, there are no major criticisms of the paradigm offered. Through the socialization process of graduate school training and the selective publication of material in the major professional journals, the dominant paradigm is placed in a secure position, according to Kuhn. In addition to the control of the intellectual environment implicit in the "normal science" stage of development, there may be a tendency for the major funding institutions to support research selectively so that the ability to secure funds is enhanced if one's research is in line with the general world view held by the funding agencies.

From the Kuhnian perspective, then, the development of "new" ideas with radically different visions of a particular scientific discipline will involve a struggle not only in the pedagogical arena but also in the research arena. How is a radical researcher to fund the research necessary to test the veracity of the assumptions implicit in the "revolutionary world view" if the funding institutions are inclined to regard such assumptions as naive, uninformed, or dangerous? A more pointed way of asking this question is: "How strongly do the research funding agencies control or inhibit the development of 'new' ideas by limiting research funding to those topics of interest only to the funding agencies themselves?" A corollary to this question, also relevant to this discussion, is: "How effective is the university in its attempts to provide institutional support for 'intellectual freedom' and 'research autonomy'?"

WHO CONTROLS CRIMINOLOGICAL RESEARCH? DILEMMAS OF GOVERNMENTAL FUNDING

Criminological research has become increasingly dependent on government funding (McCartney, 1970). The funding practices of the Law Enforcement Assistance Administration and the National Institutes of Mental Health have been discussed and criticized by Quinney (1973). The arguments he raises speak primarily to the apparent proliferation of research oriented toward the control and repression of crime rather than toward its understanding.

The relationship between the federal government's funding agencies and criminological inquiry has also been discussed by Galliher (1979: 48), who concludes that "the morality of social science seems purchased or influenced by the government." Accordingly, the funding practices of both the government and private foundations involve both direct and indirect control over the researcher's behavior. Academic researchers requesting funds from government agencies, according to Galliher, are manipulated by the conservative nature of the requests for proposals to which they may respond. Furthermore, Galliher (1979: 45) argues that the supposedly unbiased peer review panels are "stacked," in that they are composed of the "politically acceptable" and the "professionally elite" (by virtue of their affiliation with high-status universities). The recognition that "money does not come free" but instead carries with it certain limitations and controls has been discussed elsewhere (Becker and Horowitz, 1973; Record, 1967; Shils, 1973). Orlans (1967: 5) addresses this problem and leaves the researcher with succinct recommendation that not only reiterates the problem facing the researcher in this regard but also offers a possible resolution:

> If you disagree with the objectives of an agency, don't decry the morality of its staff but try to change their objectives and, in the interim, don't take their money.

As was suggested at the outset, the university *should* provide a setting wherein Orlans's resolution becomes realistically possible. The university is frequently cited as committed to academic freedom, and hence researchers functioning in such an environment should feel relatively free to choose their topics based on their interests rather than other outside factors. In reality, however, the academic institutions in the United States seem to have lost a considerable degree of autonomy due to the proliferation of government funding agencies and private research foundations that have become interested in supporting research by university faculty.

Broadhead and Rist (1976) recognize the link between the university and government funding practices and emphasize that the objectivity of scientific investigations is confounded by academe's dependency on outside sources for funding. The problems associated with this phenomenon have been discussed elsewhere (Gouldner, 1971), and C. Wright Mills (1963: 301) warns all academically inclined researchers: "To sell yourself is to turn yourself into a commodity. A commodity does not control the market: its nominal worth is determined by what the market will offer." It is clear that if the university fails to support its research faculty and instead takes the side of the funding sources, the goal of autonomy in research endeavors becomes an unrealistic expectation. Some potential problems resulting from this loss of autonomy are discussed elsewhere (Longmire and Vito, 1980).

THE GATEKEEPING PROBLEM: GAINING ACCESS TO DATA

Even if the explicit control over scientific research via funding arrangements can be avoided, the fact still remains that access to necessary data is often not possible without the consent of government representatives. Broadhead and Rist (1976) acknowledge the existence of the "gatekeeping" phenomenon in social science research in general and further criticize academic institutions for failing to take a concerted stance against such control.

The gatekeeping problem is particularly relevant to criminological research where access to populations of known criminals requires the approval of agency officials. The decision not to allow researchers to engage freely in research in correctional institutions has been cited by Cressey (1968) as one of several techniques that leaves the correctional administrator with an easy criticism of negative findings. In this regard, such findings can be mitigated by invoking one or more of the "vocabularies of adjustment" available to the correctional personnel, such as the argument that "there are too many complex variables which were not controlled in the study" (Cressey, 1968: 360). Along similar lines, Ward and Kassebaum (1966) warn that consistently negative evaluation results in the area of corrections might lead to a strengthening of the gatekeeping activity in correctional institutions by a proliferation of in house evaluations in lieu of external studies of correctional effectiveness.

Access to official records such as the Federal Bureau of Investigation's criminal history data (Rap Sheets) is limited to the law enforcement community, and unless a researcher can become aligned with a criminal justice agency willing to request the Rap Sheets, access to such data is not possible. In a recently reported incident (Carroll and Knerr, n.d.: 223), a Ph.D. candidate had to abandon a dissertation project because of this restriction.

The answer to the question "Who controls criminological research?" is complex and not without serious implications. Through funding practices and restrictive research policies, government agencies appear to have significant manipulative power over the social science disciplines. Useem (1976) assesses the impact of government financing on anthropology, economics, political science, and psychology and concludes that there is little support for the hypothesis that the government is primarily concerned with legitimizing itself through selective funding practices. However, the implications of these findings must not be generalized to the discipline of criminology without more intensive inquiry. This warning takes on special relevance if one acknowledges the argument raised by Quinney (1973) that government control over data and funding has contributed to the technologically oriented tendencies characteristic of the criminological discipline today. The fact that data sets are accessible to some researchers but remain inaccessible to others is revealed in the following note accompanying a recent article co-authored by Greenberg, Kessler, and Logan (1979: 843):

> We thank the Uniform Crime Reporting Division of the F.B.I. for supplying data on arrest rates and crime rates to Charles Logan. We are also

grateful to the F.B.I. for refusing to give David Greenberg the same data, thereby making this collaboration possible. We wish to note with concern, however, the danger to scholarly inquiry posed by this sort of selectivity in the release of data by government agencies.

The present research represents an attempt to ascertain how wide spread such problems actually are and to see whether or not there is any reason to believe that the funding agencies and gatekeepers of data selectively choose projects so as to constitute a systematic discrimination against research contrary to the dominant criminological world view. Exactly what topics fall under the rubric of the "new criminology" is not clear. Cressey (1978) notes that there have been several "new" criminologies offered in the evolution of the criminological enterprise. These have ranged from the genetic theories advanced by Schlapp and Smith (1928) to the Marxist theories of Taylor et al. (1973). For the present study, no attempt is made to restrict attention to any one of these substantive areas. Instead, whether or not one's research is "radical" or "new" is left for the researcher to decide.

DATA SET

Data used to examine these issues were collected as part of a more general study of ethical concerns facing contemporary criminological researchers. In 1980, a 10 percent sample was drawn from the *1978-1979 Membership Directory of the American Society of Criminology*. The sampling process employed involved a purely random process of selection, whereby 211 names were selected from the 2,112 names listed in the directory. A questionnaire was mailed to each of the persons selected asking them about a variety of ethical issues. The respondents were in formed that their participation was totally voluntary and that their anonymity would be assured. Following two waves of mailing, 142 completed and usable questionnaires were returned, thus constituting a response rate of approximately 67 percent. Of the remaining 69 questionnaires, 20 were either not returned or were returned by non-English-speaking American Society of Criminology members. There appears to be no reason to believe that the remaining persons who were contacted but did not return their completed questionnaires represent any select group; thus, their nonresponse should not result in any systematic omissions in the data.

Although there were numerous items in the survey instrument, the present analysis is restricted to two sections of the questionnaire which

TABLE 1.1 Number of Respondents Who Reported that They Were Denied Funding or Access to Data Due to "Radical" Nature of Their Proposed Research

Denied	No		Yes	
	%	(n)	%	(n)
Funding	79	(87)	21	(23)
Access to Data	74	(82)	26	(28)
Number of different respondents reporting some sort of denial	60	(66)	40	(44)

asked the respondents whether or not they had, in their opinion, ever been denied funding or access to data "because the nature of [their] research was 'radically' different from the mainstream perspectives." If any responded affirmatively to either of these questions, they were asked to provide a description of the nature of the proposed research, the funding source or data source involved, and any further elaboration about the incident(s) desired.

It should be further noted that the present analysis is restricted to those respondents who reported that they had been active in criminological research at some time during the five years prior to the survey (n = 110). It is interesting to note that approximately 23 percent (n = 32) of the total sample were not actively engaged in research during this period. Why they had not engaged in any research is unknown. It is possible that their nonparticipation is a result of some of the ideological pressures being examined here; however, data necessary to test the validity of this possibility are not available at this time.

Data presented in Table 1.1 show that while there were some respondents (n = 8) who reported experiencing both kinds of problems, the majority of those who were denied funding or access to data only reported singular events. Thus, while there were 51 cases of alleged discrimination (23 involving funding practices and 28 involving data access problems), there were only 44 different respondents involved in these incidents. The kinds of projects involving dual problems are described in the note to Table 1.2.

RESULTS AND DISCUSSION

Table 1.1 presents the data necessary to ascertain how frequently criminological researchers are confronted with either of the problems under study. The great majority of criminological researchers surveyed do not report any experience with either selective funding or selective access to data as a result of the nature of their research. Only 21 percent of the respondents reported that they were not funded because of the nature of their research, and 26 percent felt that the radical nature of their research was influential in their not being given access to necessary data sources. Obviously, the subjective nature of this question is problematic. What constitutes research "radically different from the mainstream perspectives" is a question which will be discussed in more detail below. However, the fact that approximately 40 percent of the respondents were, from their perspective, not able to conduct their desired research because of its radical nature tends to lend some support to the argument that there are gatekeeping practices and selective funding patterns in operation. More information about whether or not those researchers who are members of a "new criminology" group are simply not requesting funding or are not researching in areas needing access to some data set capable of being restricted is needed. The data set currently being analyzed does not allow us to examine this question.

The assessment of exactly what kinds of research endeavors were not funded or given access to data is more difficult than the rather straightforward assessment of a frequency distribution. Of the 44 respondents who reported difficulty in one or both of these areas, I was able to identify five general areas descriptive of the varied responses. The projects which are alleged to have been the victims of some form of funding discrimination or selective gatekeeping involve the following kinds of inquiries:

(1) evaluations of specific components of the criminal or juvenile justice system;
(2) studies examining the political and/or economic structure as an independent variable and some component of the criminal justice system or crime as the dependent variable (e.g., penal practices, police behavior, crime rate);
(3) studies involving research subjects who were perceived by the researcher as "radically deviant" from the more traditionally funded research (e.g., families of homicide victims, parents of youths who "overdosed" on drugs);
(4) research examining the biochemical makeup of criminals and/or victims; and

TABLE 1.2 Descriptive Characteristics of Research Projects Denied Funding or Access to Data Due to Their "Radical" Nature

| Category | Denied | | | | Number of | |
| | Funding | | Access | | Different Respondents | |
	%	(n)	%	(n)	%	(n)
1 Evaluations of system	9	(2)	50	(14)	34*	(15)
2 Political/ economic structure	43	(10)	14	(4)	32	(14)
3 Sensitive subjects	9	(2)	25	(7)	14*	(6)
4 Biological research	26	(6)	7	(2)	14*	(6)
5 Drug treatment exp.	13	(3)	4	(1)	6*	(3)
Total	100	(23)	100	(28)	100	(44)

* These figures represent the categories where some of the respondents reported that they had been denied both funding and access to data. There was one such case in Category 1, three such cases in Category 3, two such cases in Category 4, and one such case in Category 5.

  (5) research involving the use of drug-related treatment experiments (non-evaluative in nature).

The specific patterns of selective funding and data accessibility reported in Table 1.2 demonstrate that the Category 2 projects (political/ economic independent variable) were most heavily discriminated against by the funding institutions, and the Category 1 projects (system evaluations) were most heavily discriminated against in the gatekeeping of data. The more general implications of these findings will be discussed in greater detail following the examination of other patterns revealed in Table 1.2.

A close examination of these data shows that there is some validity to the sociobiological criminologists' claim that funding opportunities for their research are not widespread. Twenty-six percent of those who reported a funding denial due to the radical nature of their research were investigating some sociobiologically related phenomenon. If one were to combine the cases in Category 4 (drug-related treatment experiments) with this more specific group of studies, the apparent discrimination against biologically or chemically related research endeavors becomes more significant. If the cases in Categories 4 and 5 are similar enough to warrant such a combination, 39 percent of the research projects denied funding and 20 percent of the projects denied either funding or data access can be identified as being of a biochemical basis. Since this research area is one of the "new criminologies" discussed by Cressey (1978) and is one of the taboos discussed in Sagarin (1980b), there seems to be some support for the argument that this kind of research falling outside the dominant criminological paradigm indeed meets discrimination in the funding arena and in the general research arena.

The fact that 25 percent of those projects denied access to data fall into Category 3 is not surprising, nor is it necessarily indicative of any selectivity based on the new criminological orientation of the research. One ought to expect that studies attempting to gain access to respondents and/or data sets that include crime victims, parents of overdose cases, and other sensitive areas will be met with some caution by the respondents. These cases constituted only 14 percent of all projects denied; thus, the implications of such practices are not overwhelming. Perhaps the admonishment given by Sagarin (1980a: 16) that researchers interested in sensitive areas should "Go slowly, this is ground fraught with potential danger" applies to these projects.

Perhaps the most noteworthy finding reported in Table 1.2 is the fact that the subject areas most frequently resulting in some kind of denial involved projects falling into Categories 1 and 2. Sixty-six percent of all projects denied either funding or data accessibility were engaged in either systems evaluations (34 percent) or political/economic analysis of the system (32 percent). A closer review of those cases in Category 1 reveals that of the 15 different cases involved in systems evaluation, 10 of the respondents reported that the nature of their proposed research evaluation involved critical examinations of the system's components. Examples of such projects include evaluations of police use of deadly force, studies of judicial encouragement of plea negotiations, prosecutorial practices in white-collar crime cases compared to street crime cases, and the evaluation of inmate victimization rates as a function of the prison's social climate. Given the focus of such proposed research, it is little wonder that this kind of project constituted 50 percent of all of those projects where access to the data necessary to conduct their research was denied. The gatekeeping phenomenon seems to be at work in these cases. While they do not necessarily fall into the Marxist version of new criminology, they are clearly involved in areas outside the pure scientific tradition of traditional criminology.

The fact that 43 percent of those projects denied funding due to the alleged radical nature of their research involved investigations of the political/economic climate and their relationship to crime and criminal justice lends considerable support to the argument that the Marxist brand of new criminology is subject to discrimination in the funding arena. These cases include efforts to ascertain whether or not the severity of penal sanctions is a function of the economic structure, whether or not there is more autonomy of the legal system in socialist versus capitalist economic systems, and whether or not the selective enforcement of the law is a product of the political structure. While these topics varied considerably in the specific focus of their interests, that they have a Marxist underpinning is beyond debate. The fact that such a large proportion of those projects alleging that they were denied funding because of the "radical" nature of their research come from Category 2 lends great support to the argument that there is discrimination against the politically critical research in the funding arena.

If one combines the cases in Categories 1 and 2 due to their mutually critical nature, the charge of discrimination is even stronger. It appears from these findings that if one's research proposal focuses on the general political/economic structure, the funding agencies will not fund it; if the research involves a critical examination of one or more of the system's components, whether it is funded or not is of little concern, because gatekeepers of the data will not allow access, thus discouraging research of this nature. The ability to conduct research critical of the existing system of criminal justice is obviously going to be quite difficult in this environment.

PROSPECTS FOR A NEW CRIMINOLOGY

The fact that the two general areas receiving the most selective attention in the funding and gatekeeping arenas both fall into the realm of one of the new criminologies discussed by Cressey (1978) is alarming but not surprising. In light of the scientific growth process advanced by Kuhn (1970), it appears that there are indeed barriers to the development of perspectives and methodologies critical of the dominant criminological practices. Before we answer the question whether or not new criminology is being greeted with open arms or closed doors, more research is needed. However, the implications to be drawn from this study do not look good for the new criminology researcher.

Whether or not universities can provide the necessary insulation from these restrictive practices and make their claim for intellectual freedom more than an empty motto remains to be seen. It is unfortunate that of the 44 respondents who reported some problem in their efforts to acquire funds or data, all but three were employed in a university setting. The three nonacademic researchers accounted for all of those who were denied funding because they proposed to engage in drug-related treatment experiments. The long-range implications of these findings, in light of the shrinking governmental support for criminological research in general, remains to be seen.

REFERENCES

BECKER, H. and I. L. HOROWITZ (1972) "Radical politics and sociological research: observations on methodology and ideology." Amer. J. of Sociology 78: 48-66.

BROADHEAD, R. S. and R. C. RIST (1976) "Gatekeepers and the social control of social research." Social Problems 23: 325-336.

CARROLL, J. D. and C. R. KNERR (n.d.) "Confidentiality of social science research sources and data." Unpublished report of research project sponsored by the American Political Science Association and funded by the Russell Sage Foundation. (Copy available from the author.)

CRESSEY, D. (1978) "Criminological theory, social science, and the repression of crime." Criminology 16: 171-191.

——— (1968) "The nature and effectiveness of correctional techniques," in L. Hazelrigg (ed.) Prisons Within Society. Garden City, NY: Doubleday.

GALLIHER, J. F. (1979) "Government research funding and purchased virtue: some examples from criminology." Crime and Social Justice, Spring/Summer: 44-50.

GEIS, G. and R. MEIER (1978) "Looking backward and forward: criminologists on criminology as a career." Criminology 16: 273-288.

GORDON, R. A. (1980) "Research on IQ, race, and delinquency: taboo or not taboo?" pp. 37-66 in E. Sagarin (ed.) Taboos in Criminology. Beverly Hills, CA: Sage.

GOULDNER, A. W. (1971) The Coming Crisis of Western Sociology. New York: Avon.

GREENBERG, D. F., R. C. KESSLER, and C. H. LOGAN (1979) "A panel model of crime rates and arrest rates." Amer. Soc. Rev. 44: 843-850.

HENSON, S. D. (1980) "Female as totem, female as taboo: an inquiry into the freedom to make connections," pp. 67-80 in E. Sagarin (ed.) Taboos in Criminology. Beverly Hills, CA: Sage.

INCIARDI, J. and H. SIEGAL (1981) "Whoring around: some comments on deviance research in the private sector." Criminology 19: 165-184.

JEFFERY, C. R. (1980) "Sociobiology and criminology: the long lean years of the unthinkable and the unmentionable," pp. 115-124 in E. Sagarin (ed.) Taboos in Criminology. Beverly Hills, CA: Sage.

KARMEN, A. (1980) "Race, inferiority, crime, and research taboos," pp. 81-114 in E. Sagarin (ed.) Taboos in Criminology. Beverly Hills, CA: Sage.

KUHN, T. (1970) The Structure of Scientific Revolutions. Chicago: Univ. of Chicago Press.

LEVIN, M. E. (1980) "Science with taboos: an inherent contradiction," pp. 23-36 in E. Sagarin (ed.) Taboos in Criminology. Beverly Hills, CA: Sage.

LONGMIRE, D. R. and G. F. VITO (1980) "Expectations and anomie: the coming out of the fledgling criminologist." Presented at the 32nd Annual Meetings of the American Society of Criminology, San Francisco, November 5-9.

McCARTNEY, J. L. (1970) "On being scientific: changing styles of presentation of sociological research." Amer. Sociologist 5: 30-35.

MILLS, C. W. (1963) "The social role of the intellectual," in I. L. Horowitz (ed.) Power, Politics, and People: The Collected Essays of C. Wright Mills. New York: Oxford Univ. Press.

ORLANS, H. (1967) "Ethical problems in the relations of research sponsors and investigators," pp. 3-24 in G. Sjoberg (ed.) Ethics, Politics, and Social Research. Cambridge: Schenkman.

PLATT, T. (1974) "Prospects for a radical criminology in the United States." Crime and Social Justice, Spring/Summer: 2-10.

QUINNEY, R. (1973) Critique of Legal Order. Boston: Little, Brown.

RECORD, J. C. (1967) "The research institute and the pressure group," pp. 25-49 in G. Sjoberg (ed.) Ethics, Politics, and Social Research. Cambridge: Schenkman.

SAGARIN, E. (1980a) "Taboo subjects and taboo viewpoints in criminology," pp. 7-22 in E. Sagarin (ed.) Taboos in Criminology. Beverly Hills, CA: Sage.

——— (1980b) Taboos in Criminology. Beverly Hills, CA: Sage.

SCHLAPP, M. and E. SMITH (1928) The New Criminology. New York: Boni and Liveright.

SHILS, E. (1973) "Muting the social sciences at Berkeley." Minerva 2: 290-295.

TAYLOR, I., P. WALTON, and J. YOUNG (1973) The New Criminology: For a Social Theory of Deviance. New York: Harper & Row.

USEEM, M. (1976) "State production of social science knowledge: patterns in government financing of academic social science research." Amer. Soc. Rev. 41: 613-629.

WARD, D. and G. KASSEBAUM (1966) "On biting the hand that feeds." Presented at the 61st Annual Meetings of the American Sociological Association, Miami Beach, FL. Also reprinted in Weiss, C. (ed.), Evaluating Action Programs: Readings in Social Action and Education. Beverly Hills, CA: Sage.

II

THE NEED TO BREAK THE MOLD

Harold E. Pepinsky

Indiana University

2

TOWARD A SCIENCE OF CONFINEMENT, OUT OF THE FALLACY OF THE COUNTERROLL, IN CRIMINOLOGY

We in criminology have been preoccupied with "moral statistics" since Quetelet's *Sur l'homme* appeared in 1835. Today, practically every layperson and criminologist readily assumes that crime statistics measure legally defined depravity, or that if they do not, they should. Whether the calling of the criminologist is to develop knowledge of crime and criminality or apply it, or both, we practically all assume that crime and criminality are supremely worthy of study because they hurt people.

Today, it is standard in criminal justice texts, and common in criminology texts, to introduce students to the wealth of information about dark figures, or hidden crime, and about attempts to estimate its size or its trends. The current norm appears traceable to the President's Commission on Law and Enforcement and Administration of Justice (1967). The commission was the criminological manifestation of the "bigger and better" preoccupation of the Johnson administration's Great Society. It began its lead report with the measurement issues and introduced results of the first three major victimization studies. The President's Commission, in turn, had been caught up in the wake of the 1958

AUTHOR'S NOTE: A version of this chapter was presented at the 33rd Annual Meetings of the American Society of Criminology, Washington, D.C., November 1981. I am grateful for a weekend seminar with Harold B. and Pauline N. Pepinsky, during the genesis of this chapter, and to Graeme R. Newman and Mark Robarge for substantial help in revision.

revision of the FBI's Uniform Crime Reporting procedure, which was preceded (e.g., Gruenhut, 1951; Sellin, 1951) and followed (e.g., Robinson, 1966; Wolfgang, 1963) by scathing criticism of the inaccuracy of the FBI reports.

It is true that each statistic has had its defenders in all periods who, like Beattie (1960), draw comfort from stable patterns within crime or criminality data. This chapter argues first that since reliability of measures is an index of *failure* of social control, such assurances should be of little comfort to the criminological community. Moreover, the introduction of new measures like those of victimization has added confusion to criminological inquiry.

As matters stand, unless criminologists redefine their object of inquiry, they will remain incapable of using their data to generate knowledge of how to control crime or criminality. It will be argued that by defining measures of crime and criminality as indices of confinement —as indices of how people *respond* to social disputes (Parnell, 1978)— we can manage to put our data to practical use.

THE SCIENTIFIC IMPORTANCE
OF BEING PRACTICAL

The issue of what to do about impractical definitions of criminological measures should be of concern even to avowedly value-neutral criminologists. What control is to the practitioner, significance is to the value-free methodologist. If, as now appears to be the case (see Pepinsky, 1980a), any single estimate of whether crime or criminality has gone up or down has a fifty/fifty chance of being wrong because the index is subject to periodic bias, the researcher has as great a problem of achieving control as does the practitioner. Even stable patterns across data sets are subject to preponderance of common bias. This was Sutherland's (1940) thesis about theories relating crime to poverty. With the availability of data from self-report studies and from studies of white-collar crime, confusion has multiplied on whether the poor are more crime-prone or violent than the rich. When you stop to consider that practically every theory of criminality rests on its relation to poverty (Pepinsky, 1976: 108-110), Sutherland's critique is devastating to our field. We might know a lot about criminality, but as far as we know, we might just as well know nothing. We may well have a whole storehouse of theoretically meaningless data. In statisticians' terms, affirming the direction of a trend in crime or criminality amounts to affirming a null hypothesis.

Criminologists cannot escape the statisticians' assumption that knowledge based on affirming null hypotheses is knowledge of no significance. Put another way, when a single data set cannot resolve a theoretical controversy, physicists long ago learned to regard issues addressed by the researcher as "trivial." If knowledge grows beyond idiosyncratic description, it does so by falsifying a belief that really matters to the scientific community. That is what makes an experiment "critical." Performing critical experiments is what thoughtful people like Weber (1946) and Popper (1963, 1965) have described as the scientific calling. Criminologists of all persuasions have a vital stake in achieving control over their subject matter.

REQUISITES OF CONTROL

In all the debate over what "social control" means, the inextricable link between control of any kind and measurement gets lost. The link is both necessary and troublesome. Whether control is attainable rests on how the matter to be controlled is defined. To make the issues clear, it helps to get to the etymological root of "control."

The Late Latin origin of "control" is "contrarotulus," or "counter-roll" or "counter register." "Contrarotulus" and "contrarotulator" ("controller") were "certainly used" in 1220 in England, and probably earlier (Hunnisett, 1981; for published foundations for these conclusions, see Hunnisett, 1961a, 1961b). The earliest cited keeper of counter-rolls was the English sheriff, who began keeping copies of the Coroner's Roll in the early thirteenth century. Current wisdom is that the counter-rolls were ineffective as contributors to the accuracy of coroners' records (Hunnisett, 1981).

In theory the counterroll had three basic requisites of control:

(1) measurement against an arbitrary standard of need for action,
(2) action hypothesized more likely than not to move the measured trend in a preferred direction, and
(3) repetition of the measurement to see whether the trend has shifted as hypothesized.

Methodologically, achieving control requires that the normally pursued objective of inductive understanding be turned on its head. While the social scientist might ordinarily seek to maximize repeated measure reliability to get a stable picture of social life, control over data may be said to rest on the planned *reduction* of repeated measure reliability of an index of failure of control. Consider, for example, what might constitute achievement of control over Hirschi's (1969) finding that less parentally controlled children are more prone than others to delinquency. If the finding has even theoretical significance, it implies conjectures about what has not yet been found—conjectures that are subject to empirical refutation. When parental control changes in a population, so should rates of self-reported delinquency. The finding implies the hypothesis that official delinquency rates for the entire population will be minimized as parental bond scores regress toward the mean. It also implies that the population rate of official delinquency will decline across populations or through time, as the correlation between parental bonds and self-reported delinquency across families is reduced. By either criterion, control would be achieved by reducing stability of correlations between bonds and delinquency.

In the case of the death rolls, failure of covariance between the contents of the coroner's register and the sheriff's counterregister would imply a need for control. Corrective action might take the form of replacing the coroner. The greater the increase in covariance between the two registers after the replacement, the better the control achieved. So the theory goes.

The Fallacy of the Counterroll

Suppose it were the sheriff who cheated or was neglectful in keeping the counterroll? If the sheriff desisted after the coroner had been replaced, control would be achieved for the wrong reason. If the sheriff and the new coroner agreed to split bribes and kept the registers accordingly, control would be illusory. As every resourceful bureaucrat knows, an organization has conventional limits within which the bureaucrat is relatively immune from outside scrutiny of records. Given that the counterroll is as prone to error as the roll, a discrepancy may point to a need for control, but it does not indicate how to achieve it. Meanwhile, no comfort can be drawn from a failure of discrepancy. It is fallacious to treat the counterroll as a standard of control. The elemental control device has an elemental flaw.

The fallacy has counterparts in contemporary measurement in criminology.

The Fallacy in Measuring Crime—An Illustration

It has been found both that police offense rates understate crime according to victim survey figures and that victimization rates understate crime according to police records (Pepinsky 1980a: 147). Given the possibility of overreporting, each becomes a flawed criterion of the validity of the other (Pepinsky, 1980a: 93-95, 120-125).

Meanwhile, from 1973 through 1978, victim survey rates of household burglary declined nationwide by over 6.2 percent, while police-produced residential burglary rates increased by 24 percent. Depending on relative trends in underreporting both exclusive and common to the two measures, the true trend in burglary may either be upward or downward for all that can be known. Even if the two trends are parallel, the possibility remains that the trend is common error.

Another Illustration

Rest your faith in measures accounting for discrimination in legislation (Sutherland, 1940) and enforcement (Chambliss and Nagasawa, 1969), and controlling for sex and age, the average American who has never been locked up in jail is about as crooked and hurtful as the average inmate (or even more so, see Reiman, 1979). On the other hand, rest your faith in the discretion of public officials, and we need to be more determined about punishing offenders with prior records of punishment, who are the real offenders (see Kramer's analysis, forthcoming).

Thus, locking up more offenders identified as habitual, as currently in the United States, is either a failure or a success in social control, depending on what measure—that of discrimination or that by officials —is designated the standard of control.

Schizophrenia of the Fallacy of the Counterroll

The fallacy confronting criminologists puts them in what Bateson (1980: 127-142; 1972: 279-308) called a "double bind." On the one hand, criminologists are open to criticism for failure to develop knowledge of how to reduce indices of crime and criminality. On the other hand, if they develop such knowledge, they are open to criticism for having reduced a false index of crime and criminality.

Bateson discovered that one response to the double bind in many species of animals—people included—is schizophrenia. If we look at criminologists collectively as a form of animal organism, it is fair to say that life with the fallacy of the counterroll has produced the symptoms of schizophrenia in the criminological body. What each faction of criminologists knows about controlling crime and criminals rests in part in assuming that knowledge of competing factions is detached from reality. For instance, knowledge of how social forces affect crime according to victim survey data rests in part on the assumption that knowledge of how forces affect police offenses-known rates is false or trivial, while offenses-known adherents dismiss what is known from contradictory victimization trends. Within the overall realm of this circular logic, nobody knows anything because everyone knows something, which is clearly crazy.

BEYOND SCHIZOPHRENIA

Members of some species of animals—humans included—have demonstrated themselves capable of resolving double binds without resort to schizophrenia. Bateson observed the alternative resolution in some porpoises. These porpoises were initially given fish for repeating behavior they happened to be performing when the trainer blew a whistle. In the next set of trials, the fish and whistle were withheld for repeating the same behavior. Instead, the whistle and fish came for doing something else. In successive trials, all behavior that had previously been awarded earned no rewards. This produced a double bind in the porpoises much like that of criminologists, who may initially be rewarded for learning how to control one index of crime or criminality only to be told that that control is no grounds for reward in successive trials.

After growing signs of disturbance, some porpoises eventually learned to enter each set of trials by displaying a spirited burst of unprecedented behaviors until rewarded.

Bateson described the breakthrough as movement to a third level of learning. At the first level, the porpoise learns to do something, as opposed to nothing, for the reward. At the second level, the porpoise learns to distinguish that one behavior (the currently rewarded) is preferable to another (the formerly rewarded). At the third level, the porpoise learns to combine previously discriminated behavior into *sets,* defined not by what the behavior is at any point in time but by when the behaviors occur over time. Generally:

> *Learning I* is *change in specificity of response* by correction of errors of choice within a set of alternatives.

> *Learning II* is *change in the process of Learning I, e.g.,* a corrective change is made in the sets of alternatives from which choice is made, or it is a change in how the sequence of experience is punctuated.

Learning III is change in the process of Learning II, e.g., a corrective change in the system of *sets* of alternatives from which choice is made [Bateson, 1980: 293].

Within criminology, Learning I was to discriminate whether a measure of crime or criminality changed as hypothesized. Learning II was to learn to discriminate between acceptable and unacceptable measures. Learning III would be to discriminate between what sets of measures have in common that is acceptable or unacceptable.

Among all measures, the equation between them and extent of unlawfulness is problematic. But if one shifts one's thinking to what it is all the measures do equally, the problem can be overcome. This movement to Learning III can also be described as resort to tautology.

As Bateson (1980) himself pointed out, tautology is the only proof of an equation, including equations between measures and things to be measured. This means that once there is room to question an equation between a measure and a thing to be controlled, either the definition of the thing to be controlled has to change or the measure abandoned as a standard of control.

For some, like Garfinkel (1966), it is the task of the social scientist to draw tautologies into question by examining and demystifying the taking for granted of "indexical expressions." This is a process that has led criminologists further into the double bind of crime measurement— into finding that various measures of crime and criminality draw each other into question.

It is frustrating to carry the phenomenological reduction too far. One gets the feeling that one is indeed becoming what Spiro Agnew called a nattering nabob of negativism, and the temptation to drift off into obscurity is strong.

On the other hand, it is not satisfactory to treat a measure as a true index of trends in crime or criminality just because "it is the best we've got." It is no comfort to fail to find a consistent bias in the data, when so many biases are known to occur that the accuracy of trends in the measures at any point in particular would be largely coincidental. Even homicide trends are subject to manipulation, as by playing politics with the relative trends in offenses-known rates and arrest rates (Selke and Pepinsky, forthcoming), by varying the routine of medical examination (Maratea, 1980), or by correcting offense rates for failure of conviction of murder (Gibson and Klein, 1961, 1969). We are long past the point at which we can assume we are safer when the police report fewer offenses. And contrary to the prophecy laid down by Wilson (1975) and Van den Haag (1975), we scarcely feel safer for having offenders punished by incarceration at record rates.

Resolution of the tension between inquiry and delusion is a matter of timing. You relax your definitions of the thing to be controlled until you have no reason to doubt the equation between what you are measuring and something you seek to control, optimizing for parsimony. You are left with the foundation of what Popper (1965) has called "conjecture," or with what Kuhn (1974) has called a "paradigm," from which a body of testable theory can be generated.

Relaxing the definition of measures of crime and criminality from "unlawfulness"—a questionable equation—another definition appears of what the measures have in common, thus far without question: *Every measure of crime and criminality is an index of willingness or commitment to treating incidents or persons as in need of confinement by criminal justice employees. In brief, all may be said to be measures of "confinement."*

The state commissioner of corrections or of parole, or a probation or parole officer, or the court, or the jailer, or a law enforcement officer creates crime statistics by placing persons in custody, and often in addition, contributing to an offender's prior record as a pretext for further confinement. The complainant to the police has expressed a willingness for officials to take a matter or a person off the complainant's hands. The victim tells the victim surveyor that the incident would have been reported had the reporter believed the police capable of carrying through. The self-reported offender contributes to an index supporting the need for more pervasive crime control. All are willing or committed to have incidents or persons managed by officials.

Parnell (1978) has discovered an interesting twist on "willingness" in Oaxaca, Mexico. There, villagers gave trivial but troublesome matters to officials to distract them from other concerns. Like the porpoises who decided to have fun, the villagers decide which incidents they would rather have officials manage. As Erikson (1966) and others since (e.g., Pontell, 1979) have suggested, inertia of the capacity of the criminal justice system to confine is remarkably strong. The Oaxacan villagers Parnell describes have apparently learned to accommodate.

Leaving open the politics of deciding among forms of confinement, any of us who presume that an improvement in a measure of crime or criminality is progress implicitly presume that confinement is at issue.

"Confinement" is one definition of what crime and criminality data measure, that for now seems to be tautologous with the measures we have and use. Whether "confinement" is a morally acceptable topic of inquiry for criminologists, criminologists cannot adequately rest on the epistemic ground of studying unlawful behavior, where we have so long stayed to no good end.

CONCLUSION

Control transforms a field into a discipline. Criminology sorely needs discipline. By design or by coincidence—it matters not—our measures highlight our plight by dealing so manifestly with social control. Insofar as we can agree that ours is the study of confinement, we are capable of becoming a true interdiscipline. It remains to be seen whether we have the will to shift our object of inquiry to suit scientific needs.

Bateson held out the possibility of a fourth level of learning:

> *Learning IV* would be *change in Learning III*, but probably does not occur in any adult living organism on this earth. Evolutionary process has, however, created organisms whose ontogeny brings them to Level III. The combination of phylogenesis with ontogenesis, in fact, achieves Level IV [1980: 293].

As Level III is to individuals, so Level IV can become to species. Among species of scholars, Level IV corresponds to what Kuhn (1974) has called "paradigm shift." As one member of the criminological community, I have redefined my field of inquiry as that of the study of confinement. But among my community, one person's shift does not change the field.

Criminologists studying unlawfulness have been locked into schizophrenia since measures of arrest came to compete with those of correction more than a century ago. I would like to think that we are reaching the point at which our schizophrenia is no longer tolerable to the criminological community as a whole. If I am right, we stand at the same point as physicists of a century ago. Caught in a double bind between laws of matter and laws of energy, they began to exchange a variety of ideas as to how matter and energy might be redefined to be forms of the same thing.

Certainly there are many criminologists who, on the other hand, cannot rest content with studying unlawfulness and yet who cannot accept theirs as the study of confinement. Accordingly, one may expect the proposal of a number of resolutions other than mine of the double bind of criminological measurement.

At this point, the species of criminologists moves from the personal realm of ontogeny of individual redefinitions of our field to the phylogeny of emergence of one redefinition as predominant over others. No single criminologist among us can determine the outcome of this contention of definitions. But each criminologist can help bring on the eventual resolution by attending to the task of redefinition. It is only when enough of us care to try curing our schizophrenia one way that a new criminological discipline will emerge some way.

REFERENCES

BATESON, G. (1980) Mind and Nature: A Necessary Unity. New York: Bantam.
——— (1972) Steps to an Ecology of Mind. New York: Ballantine.
BEATTIE, R. H. (1960) "Criminal statistics in the United States." J. of Criminal Law, Criminology and Police Science 51: 49-65.
CHAMBLISS, W. and R. D. NAGASAWA (1969) "On the validity of official statistics: a comparison of white, black, and Japanese high school boys." J. of Research in Crime and Delinquency 6: 71-77.
ERIKSON, K. T. (1966) Wayward Puritans: A Study in the Sociology of Deviance. New York: John Wiley.
GARFINKEL, H. (1966) Studies in Ethnomethodology. Englewood Cliffs, NJ: Prentice-Hall.
GIBSON, E. and KLEIN, S. (1969) Home Office Research Studies, No. 3: Murder, 1957-1968. London: Her Majesty's Stationery Office.
——— (1961) Home Office Studies in the Causes of Delinquency and the Treatment of Offenders, No. 4: Murder—A Home Office Research Report. London: Her Majesty's Stationery Office.
GRUENHUT, M. (1951) "Statistics in criminology." J. of the Royal Statistical Society 114: 149-150.
HIRSCHI, T. (1969) Causes of Delinquency. Berkeley: Univ. of California Press.
HUNNISETT, R. F. (1981) Private Correspondence from Records Office, Chancery Lane, London (March).
——— (1961a) Bedfordshire Coroner's Rolls. Bedfordshire, England: Bedfordshire Historical Records Society Publications.
——— (1961b) The Medieval Coroner. Cambridge, England: Cambridge Univ. Press.
KITSUSE, J. I., and A. V. CICOUREL (1963) "A note on the uses of official statistics." Social Problems 11: 132-139.
KRAMER, R. C. (forthcoming) "From 'Habitual offenders' to 'career criminals': the historical construction and development of criminal categories." Law and Human Behavior (special issue, "Contemporary Lessons from Historical Research").
KUHN, T. S. (1974) The Structure of Scientific Revolution. Chicago: Univ. of Chicago Press.

MARATEA, C. (1980) Telephone interview, October 6. (Administrator, Hamilton County, Ohio, Coroner's Office.

ORTEGA Y GASSETT, J. (1957) Revolt of the Masses. New York: Norton.

PARNELL, P. C. (1978) "Village or state? competitive legal systems in a Mexican judicial district," pp. 315-350 in L. Nader and H. F. Todd, Jr. (eds.) The Disputing Process: Law in Ten Societies. New York: Columbia Univ. Press.

PEPINSKY, H. E. (1980a) Crime Control Strategies: An Introduction to the Study of Crime. New York: Oxford Univ. Press.

——— (1980b) "On handling contradictions between dynastic tradition and Marxist humanism: the new criminal law in Communist China as an effort to legitimize the post-Mao state," pp. 180-198 in Tsai Wei-ping (ed.) Struggling for Change in Mainland China: Challenges and Implications. Taipei: Institute of International Relations.

——— (1976) Crime and Conflict: A Study of Law and Society. New York: Academic Press.

PONTELL, H. N. (1979) "Deterrence and system capacity: an ecological analysis of crime, punishment and court caseloads." Presented at American Society of Criminology annual meeting, Philadelphia, November.

POPPER, K. (1965) Conjectures and Refutations: The Growth of Scientific Knowledge. New York: Harper & Row.

——— (1963) The Open Society and Its Enemies (2 vols.). Princeton: Princeton Univ. Press.

President's Commission on Law Enforcement and Administration of Justice (1967) The Challenge of Crime in a Free Society. Washington, DC: Government Printing Office.

REIMAN, J. H. (1979) The Rich Get Richer and the Poor Get Prison. New York: John Wiley.

ROBINSON, S. M. (1966) "A critical view of the Uniform Crime Reports." Michigan Law Rev. 64: 1031-1054.

SELKE, W. L. and H. E. PEPINSKY (forthcoming) "The politics of fear." Law and Human Behavior (special issue, "Contemporary Lessons from Historical Research").

SELLIN, J. T. (1951) "The significance of records of crime." Law Q. Rev. 67: 489-504.

SUTHERLAND, E. H. (1940) "Is 'white-collar crime' crime?" Amer. Soc. kev. 5: 1-12.

TAYLOR, I., P. WALTON, J. YOUNG (1973) The New Criminology. London: Routledge & Kegan Paul.

VAN DEN HAAG, E. (1975) Punishing Criminals: Concerning a Very Old and Painful Question. New York: Basic Books.

WEBER, M. (1946) "Science as a vocation," pp. 129-156 in H. H. Gerth and C. W. Mills (eds.) From Max Weber: Essays in Sociology. New York: Oxford Univ. Press.

WILSON, J. Q. (1975) Thinking about Crime. New York: Basic Books.

WOLFGANG, M. E. (1963) "Uniform Crime Reports: a critical appraisal." Pennsylvania Law Rev. 111: 708-738.

III

NEW PREMISES—FROM THE GENERAL TO THE SPECIFIC

Robert M. Bohm
Jacksonville State University

3

CAPITALISM, SOCIALISM, AND CRIME

Two propositions asserted by Marxist criminologists are (1) that "socialism" is the inevitable successor to "capitalism" and (2) that "socialism" is a panacea for crime (Quinney, 1977: 151, 1975: 199; Center for Research on Criminal Justice, 1977: 197; Wright, 1973: 337; Chambliss, 1976: 9; Balkan et al., 1980: 316). These criminologists consider the United States as an exemplar of capitalism and accuse the uninformed or misinformed of mistakenly identifying the Soviet Union as an exemplar of socialism.

In this chapter it is suggested that the concept of capitalism neither accurately nor adequately describes the contemporary United States; that socialism, as Marx (and Engels) conceived it, is merely an antithesis to capitalism and not a synthesis or "fait accompli"; that socialism, as Marx (and Engels) conceived it, is not represented by any nation currently extant; that both concepts, as well as other concepts of "postcapitalist" alternatives, should be treated as abstractions rather than as descriptions of social systems. While the concepts are useful for heuristic purposes as ideal types, they often confuse rather than clarify discussions of social formations[1] and of praxis.

This investigation concludes (1) that socialism is *not* the inevitable successor to capitalism and (2) that socialism is *not* necessarily a

AUTHOR'S NOTE: A version of this chapter was prepared for presentation at the 1982 Annual Meeting of the Academy of Criminal Justice Sciences, Louisville, Kentucky. I would like to thank Don Des Roches and Hal Pepinsky for their generous contributions to the readability of this manuscript.

panacea for crime. It is hoped that the object or objects of radical praxis—especially the problem of crime—may be clarified and better understood.

The Concept of Capitalism Neither Accurately
Nor Adequately Describes the Contemporary United States

Is the United States an exemplar of capitalism, as Marxist criminologists apparently presume? The answer to that question ultimately depends on one's definition of capitalism. Although the term "capitalism" is said to have been coined in 1854 by W. M. Thackeray, the concept, as currently used by Marxist criminologists, was not popularized until the 1880s, when socialists employed it to describe the economic system they were attacking. The concepts of capital and capitalist had been used earlier, but in a different sense than that employed by Marxist criminologists (Gould and Kolb, 1964).

Karl Marx, with whom the concept is typically identified and to whom radical criminologists almost without exception refer, rarely, if ever, employed the concept of capitalism. He wrote about capital, capitalists, the capitalist mode of production, and bourgeois production but not capitalism. Perhaps the reason for this is that Marx never considered himself a "socialist"—that is, a member of the group that popularized the concept of capitalism in the 1880s. He employed the concept of "communist" (as in *The Communist Manifesto,* 1848[1974]) to distinguish his perspective from theirs.

Like Marx, Adam Smith, who wrote *The Wealth of Nations* (1776), the work to which the doctrines of capitalism are usually traced, never used the concept. Smith wrote about an economic policy of "laissez faire"—a concept coined in 1664 by a French businessman named Legendre in response to Colbert's question about what the government should do to help businessmen. Legendre is alleged to have answered, "Nous Laisser faire" ("Let us do it, let us alone," Durant and Durant, 1967: 72). The concept of capitalism was not popularized until over 100 years after *The Wealth of Nations* was published.

Nevertheless, the concept of capitalism has become almost synonymous with Smith's economic policy of laissez faire—that is, the policy of no government intervention in the economy—and with the economic system Marx attacked. *Webster's Dictionary,* for example, defines "capitalism" as "an economic system characterized by private or corporation ownership of capital goods, by investments that are determined by private decision rather than state control, and by prices, production, and the distribution of goods that are determined mainly in a free market." In this definition, which is typical of nominal definitions, two major indicators of capitalism are emphasized: (1) that property, especially the means of production, is privately or corporately owned, and (2) that the "economic system" is based on economic freedom or freedom of enterprise (decisions are made in a "free market"). Note that the definition explicitly excludes any state intervention in the economy.

Consequently, even if the policy of laissez faire is the distinguishing characteristic or indicator of capitalism, the United States still cannot be considered an exemplar of capitalism, especially since Roosevelt's New Deal.

Subtypes of capitalism (e.g., competitive, industrial, monopoly, welfare) have been conceived to account for historical transformations of "capitalism," including increased state intervention. Each of these subtypes, however, also implies an absence of state intervention in a portion of the economy. For example, "welfare capitalism" denotes a public welfare system entirely financed by private contributions and not government largesse.

Other descriptions of capitalism emphasize at least nine additional indicators of capitalism: (1) the predominant ownership of the means of production by one class consisting of a minority of the population; (2) workers, who comprise the majority of the population and who own almost nothing productive but their labor power; (3) the economic goals of private profit and surplus value production; (4) competition; (5) unemployment; (6) business cycles; (7) inheritance; (8) inflation; and (9) credit. While a discussion of the role that each of these indicators is presumed to play in allegedly capitalist societies like the United States is beyond the scope of this chapter,[2] a few general remarks are necessary.

First, while the contemporary United States to some extent has all of the indicators just listed, conceptual clarity requires that "capitalism" be reserved for economic systems that are entirely or primarily free of state or government intervention.

Second, regardless of whether or not one assumes that the United States is an exemplar of capitalism, the indicators listed above can characterize social formations other than capitalism.

Third, it is important to determine the criminogenic effects, if any, of each of these indicators regardless of whether the United States is considered an exemplar of capitalism. The indicators still suggest exploitive inter- or intraclass social relations which may breed crime. Capitalistic or not, these elements of the American social structure may require radical transformation.

Socialism, as Marx and Engels Conceived It, Is Merely an Antithesis to Capitalism and Not a Synthesis or a "Fait Accompli"

For Marx and Engels, socialism is only the transitional stage between capitalism and communism. It is the antithesis in a dialectical relationship in which capitalism is the thesis and communism the synthesis.

Although capitalism, for Marx and Engels, is inevitably doomed by its inherent contradictions, it is nevertheless requisite to preparing society for socialism. For example, they hold that it is through capitalism that industrialization and technology advance to the stage where socialism becomes possible. This is why socialism, as Marx and Engels conceived it, is impossible in societies that are not highly industrialized and highly technological.

When capitalism eventually succumbs either to its inherent contradictions or to radical transformation, socialism will dominate social relations and prepare society for communism, which, for Marx and Engels, is the synthesis of capitalism and socialism or the "fait accompli."[3] Socialism is not Marx's and Engel's synthesis or fait accompli, communism is. Because of its own contradictions, socialism is projected to succumb to communism much as capitalism succumbs to socialism.

As a transitional stage, socialism is necessary because it abolishes the class relation which forms the basis of capitalist production, by expropriating from the propertied class and by socializing or nationalizing land and capital (the means of production), including inherited land and capital. In short, socialism is presumed to eliminate many of the indicators of capitalism.

For Marx and Engels, a major contradiction of socialism is the necessary existence of a state which will only "wither away" under communism. Since workers comprise the majority of the population, they can gain control of the state and, through the state, the economy, by the democratic political process. A politically democratic state and socialism are not only compatible but necessary. Sherman (1972: 299) may be correct in his observation that political democracy, as we currently practice it in the United States, may be improved in a society characterized by the socialization of land, capital, and the means of production, and by economic planning directed to the fulfillment of human needs and social goals—that is, by the rise of Marxist socialism.

Ironically, some critics of socialism have apparently dismissed or missed the notions that political democracy and socialism are compatible, even inseparable, and that political democracy, as currently practiced in the United States, for example, may be improved under socialism.

Socialism, as Marx and Engels Conceived It, Is Not Represented by Any Nation Currently Extant

Many equate "socialism" with "totalitarianism," and use the Soviet Union to confirm their belief. However, as Sherman (1972: 304) explains, just because the Soviet Union may be characterized as totalitarian, it does not necessarily follow that socialism is inherently totalitarian. There are at least three important differences between the model of socialism conceived by Marx and Engels and the social formation of the Soviet Union.

First, Bolshevism was conceived by Lenin and Trotsky as a social movement that would adapt Marx's and Engel's conception of socialism to the specific time, place, and conditions that they confronted in czarist Russia. It is unlikely that Bolshevism was intended as a universal or faithful Marxist model of socialism. Second, Bolshevism differs from socialism both in the designation of the revolutionary agent in society and the specification of who will direct the society. Under socialism as Marx and Engels conceived it, the proletariat (working class) is the revolutionary agent in society and "a dictatorship of the proletariat" is who will direct it. Under Bolshevism, on the other hand, the revolutionary agent in society was both the worker and the peasant (in order to take into consideration the peculiar circumstances of czarist Russia). Society, moreover, was to be directed by a "party of the vanguard"—"a disciplined, tightly organized party of professional revolutionaries" (Mills, 1975: 140). Finally, and most important, Bolshevism also differs from socialism, as Marx and Engels conceived it, in the type of society in which it can, by definition, occur. The socialism of Marx and Engels can emerge only in advanced capitalist nations, while Bolshevism was specifically designed for a nonindustrial nation (Mills, 1975: 140).

Similarly, Stalinism, like Bolshevism, was not intended as a universal or faithful Marxist model of socialism. Stalinism, like Bolshevism, must be understood as a response to specific circumstances in the nascent Soviet Union: (1) the need to maintain social order (at any cost) in order to consolidate the revolution, (2) the need to defend the new social formation against external enemies, and (3) the need to enforce labor discipline and consumption sacrifices in order to construct heavy industry as quickly as possible (Mills, 1975: 144-145). In sum, Stalinism, like

Bolshevism, is neither the socialism of Marx and Engels nor a successor to capitalism.

Socialism, as Marx and Engels Conceived it, Is not the Inevitable Successor to Capitalism

Besides the socialism of Marx and Engels, Bolshevism, and Stalinism, numerous models of socialism have been contrived throughout history (e.g., Fourierism, Guild Socialism, Owenism, Maoism, Castroism). As in the cases of Bolshevism and Stalinism, most of these models cannot be considered possible successors to capitalism because they were or are intended for nonindustrial societies.

Contrary to assertions by some Marxist criminologists, history has demonstrated that there are other social formations that may succeed capitalism besides the socialism of Marx and Engels. Two examples are bourgeois socialism (sometimes called state socialism) and fascism.

Marx and Engels (1974: 107) wrote critically about the model of socialism that they called "conservative" or "bourgeois socialism." According to Marx and Engels (1974: 107), bourgeois socialism arises because "a part of the bourgeoisie is desirous of redressing social grievances, in order to secure the continued existence of bourgeois society." Harrington (1976: 208-209), who refers to bourgeois socialism as "state socialism," argues that it is a means by which a capitalist ruling class, intent on maintaining its hegemony in society, is able to defuse dissent (see Piven and Cloward, 1971, for a similar view).

This model of socialism, whether labeled bourgeois or state, is simply an expedient, a vehicle by which a capitalist ruling class is able to maintain its hegemony over society despite the occurrence of economic setbacks and the perpetuation of exploitation. A major difference between bourgeois socialism and the socialism of Marx and Engels is that the latter seeks the transformation of society as a whole, and therefore opposes the notion that welfare programs, isolated instances of government ownership, or the like constitute a socialist society.

At its extreme, bourgeois socialism or state socialism becomes fascism. Fascism is characterized by complete state command of the economy. It arises under certain historical conditions when the capitalist ruling class of a particular nation is threatened with imminent demise.

In short, fascism, like bourgeois socialism, is not the socialism of Marx and Engels, although it, like bourgeois socialism, is a possible successor to the contemporary social formation in the United States. Marxist socialism need not prevail.

Socialism Is not Necessarily a Panacea for Crime

There is no reason to believe, as some Marxist criminologists apparently do, that socialism is the solution to the crime problem. Indeed, there is every reason to believe that under socialism (in whatever form) where there will be "unequal distribution of goods and payments to individuals according to their work," there will be crime, though it may not be labeled as such. Crime under socialism may even play a necessary and constructive educational role (see Gordon, 1976: 209-210).

Even under a socialist transition toward communism, it is theoretically plausible to assume that there will be socially problematic behavior whether it is labeled criminal or not. Only the final movement into communism provides the conditions for a crime-free society.

A problem with most nominal definitions of communism (e.g., Webster's) is that they are indistinguishable from descriptions of socialism. They are, in other words, misleading descriptions of communism. The source of this confusion is probably Marx and Engels themselves. Marx and Engels employed the term "communism" to denote both their model of socialism and their separate model of communism in order to distinguish their program "from various utopian and social reformist groups which were known as socialists," for whom Marx and Engels had little respect (Loucks and Whitney, 1969: 67). But more precisely, Marx and Engels used the term to describe the synthesis of capitalism and socialism.

In *The German Ideology,* Marx and Engels (1970: 53) wrote:

> In communist society, where nobody has one exclusive sphere of activity but each can become accomplished in any branch he wishes, society regulates the general production and thus makes it possible for me to do one thing today and another tomorrow.

While Marx and Engels's conception of communism appears utopian or idealistic to many, it is important to understand that their communism is neither "a 'state of affairs' which is to be established" nor "an 'ideal' to which reality [will] have to adjust itself," but rather "the 'real' movement which abolishes the present state of things" (Marx and Engels, 1970: 56-57). For them, communism is immanent in the conditions underlying capitalism and socialism.

It is problematic whether an industrial society can or will become communist. Communism entails (1) a great increase in production, (2) efficient planning, (3) increased education and research, (4) no unemployment, (5) no wasteful advertising, (6) no monopoly misallocation, and (7) no military spending (Sherman, 1972). As to increased production, Marx and Engels (1970: 56) write:

> Communism is only possible as the act of the dominant peoples "all at once" and simultaneously, which presupposes the universal development of productive forces and the world intercourse bound up with communism.

Increased production, in turn, presumably is made possible by increased technology and mechanization, which makes most coerced human labor unnecessary. Unemployment under communism ceases to be a problem. Production supplies people with the goods and services necessary to satisfy their "needs" without people having to labor to have their needs met. As Marcuse (1966: 231) describes, "For it is this base which has rendered possible the satisfaction of needs and the reduction of toil—it remains the very base of all forms of human freedom." Furthermore, if people are no longer compelled to labor to meet their needs, there will be greater opportunity for educational and research activity.

The problem of planning (social organization) is as important as and perhaps a more controversial requisite of communism than advances in the technological base and increased production. Under communism, it is presumed that production is "universalized," not "nationalized" as under socialism and fascism, for example. In short, a state or government, as we now know them, are unncessary under communism. Ideally, communism, like capitalism, is a world-system or stateless society. There would be no need for military spending under communism, since there would be no external enemy.

In the absence of a state or government under communism, there is some controversy as to how production would be planned and how goods and services would be distributed. With regard to the planning of production, there is a paucity of help in the literature. However, the impression is given that decisions in a communist society would be made by representatives, elected frequently by all the people, who served on a part-time basis without pay—much like Athenian democracy without slavery. In essence, these representatives would distribute goods and services to satisfy relatively homogeneous social needs. It is this homogeneity of social needs, moreover, that presumably would eliminate conflicts of interest as well as wasteful advertising and monopoly misallocation. Also, since production under communism presumably would be able to satisfy people's needs, there would be no necessary conflict between an individual's need and social needs.

Since it is believed that under communism production would satisfy all people's needs, all goods and services would be distributed "free" to people according to their needs. As Sherman (1972: 339) maintains, "Under pure communism, 'free' goods would be produced under public control and ownership, and consumed by everyone according to his desires." Sherman (1972: 353, n.4) warns, however, that "free" in this context means "zero price in the market; it does not mean free like air, since any production of goods requires use of labor and other resources and a foregone opportunity cost to society."

At least three problems with this notion of "free" distribution under communism have been posed. First, it is suggested that if all goods and services are free, demand would be insatiable, because people's needs are infinite. Consequently, supply could never meet demand. Second, it is argued that if all goods and services are free, and therefore people are not compelled to labor, they will not labor. It is assumed that human beings, by nature, are lazy. Third, it is argued that if goods and services are free—that is, without prices—planning would be difficult to accomplish and production would consequently be inefficient (Sherman, 1972: 340).

According to Sherman, a solution to these problems is "partial" rather than "full communism" in which 80-90 percent of all goods and services are free. Going further, Turgeon writes:

> It seems possible that those who would deny the eventual possibility of communist distribution tend to underestimate the growing technological potential for the creation of abundance; to overestimate the insatiability of innate consumer needs; and to underrate the possible changes in man's approach to work and life [quoted in Sherman, 1972: 352].

What about crime in communist society? Unfortunately, Marxist criminologists seldom entertain this question. They seem intent on discussing the possibility of crime only in capitalist and socialist societies. But even if life under communism were crime-free, Marxist criminologists have a lot to do to explain how to get from here to there.

CONCLUSION

It is incumbent on criminologists, especially Marxist criminologists, to stop arguing in generalities (e.g., socialism versus capitalism) and to engage in the difficult task of specifying which indicators of contemporary social formations must be changed if the problem of crime is to be resolved.

In the United States, a fundamental issue remains the conceptualization of crime. As Marxist criminologists have correctly indicated, the legal definition of crime represents only a selective and class-biased group of exploitive social relations. Excluded from this definition are all of the indicators of capitalism listed earlier, including the state. Consequently, criminologists must investigate the extent to which these indicators characterize the contemporary United States, and then the extent to which they are exploitive and thus produce crime.[4]

It may be that the indicators are not inherently exploitive, but that they imply exploitive relations only under certain conditions. In that case a determination of the criminogenic effects, if any, of each of the indicators is in order. However, at least two problems impede pursuing such a task: (1) finding and agreeing on empirical referents for the indicators, and (2) finding and agreeing on an empirical referent for crime.

An underlying problem in this regard, as in more traditional analyses, is the use of official and unofficial measures of crime. If investigators limit themselves to using official statistics, such an investigation will merely demonstrate the extent to which criminal justice activity is affected by the indicators. The use of unofficial statistics will only measure the degree of public consciousness about crime.

Another difficult task confronting criminologists is to educate the public to recognize exploitive social relations and their mystifications. For example, in the case of unemployment, assuming that unemployment is related to crime, the general public must be educated to the fact that being laid off a job is not primarily the result of "bad luck" or "God's will" but of political and economic decisions.

The choice of tasks confronting criminologists is imposing. Criminologists can continue to support and perpetuate the status quo by either working within the narrow constraints of the legal definition of crime or by speaking in generalities about capitalism, socialism, and the like. They might do better to seek a radical transformation of society, and with it the problem of crime, through a reconceptualization of the concept of crime and an investigation of the specific indicators of our contemporary social formation.

NOTES

1. The concept of "social formation" is employed in this analysis to denote a particular phase or stage in world history. Following Marx, a social formation is presumed to consist of a "mode of production" and a "superstructure." A mode of production consists of the

following interacting components: (1) the material powers of production (e.g., natural resources and the physical equipment of labor), (2) the social relations of production (e.g., private property and classes), and (3) human needs. Although there is no consensus in the literature on what is to be included in the superstructure, the family, the state, law, religion, education, the mass media, and the criminal justice system are all typically considered superstructural institutions. It is important to stress the interrelatedness of all the components of a social formation, because it is the interrelatedness of these components that ultimately separates Marxist analyses from most traditional analyses. In other words, in this analysis it is assumed that a quantitative or qualitative change in one component of a social formation will necessary alter all of the other components in that social formation.

2. It should be noted that other social institutions, such as religion, sexism, and racism, are also typically associated with capitalism. These institutions, however, while augmenting capitalist productive relations, preceded the advent of capitalism and are likely to transcend capitalist productive relations as well.

3. One wonders why the dialectical relationship ends with communism for Marx and Engels. Why doesn't communism become a new thesis that is superseded by a new antithesis and that results in a new synthesis ad infinitum?

4. A useful criterion for determining the extent of exploitation of a particular indicator is the distinction between the "exchange values" and the "use values" inherent in that indicator (see Mandel, 1976: 9-10, 1978: 593-594, 598). Those indicators lacking in use values or manifesting primarily exchange values should be included in a reconceptualization of crime.

REFERENCES

BALKAN, S., R. J. BERGER, and J. SCHMIDT (1980) Crime and Deviance in America: A Critical Approach. Belmont, CA: Wadsworth.

Center for Research on Criminal Justice (1977) The Iron Fist and the Velvet Glove. Berkeley: Center for Research on Criminal Justice.

CHAMBLISS, W. J. (1976) "Functional and conflict theories of crime: the heritage of Emile Durkheim and Karl Marx," pp. 1-28 in W. J. Chambliss and M. Mankoff (eds.) Whose Law What Order? New York: John Wiley.

DURANT, W. and A. DURANT (1967) Rousseau and Revolution. New York: Simon & Schuster.

GORDON, D. M. (1976) "Class and the economics of crime," pp. 193-214 in W. J. Chambliss and M. Mankoff (eds.) Whose Law What Order? New York: John Wiley.

GOULD, J. and W. L. KOLB [eds.] (1964) A Dictionary of the Social Sciences. New York: Free Press.

HARRINGTON, M. (1976) The Twilight of Capitalism. New York: Simon & Schuster.

LOUCKS, W. N. and W. G. WHITNEY (1969) Comparative Economic Systems. New York: Harper & Row.

MANDEL, E. (1978) Late Capitalism. London: Verso.

——— (1976) An Introduction to Marxist Economic Theory. New York: Pathfinder.

MARCUSE, H. (1966) One-Dimensional Man. Boston: Beacon.

MARX, K. and F. ENGELS (1974) The Communist Manifesto (1848). New York: Washington Square Press.

—— (1970) The German Ideology. New York: International Publishers.
MILLS, C. W. (1975) The Marxists. New York: Dell.
PIVEN, F. F. and R. A. CLOWARD (1971) Regulating the Poor: The Functions of Public Welfare. New York: Vintage.
QUINNEY, R. (1977) Class, State and Crime. New York: David McKay.
—— (1975) "Crime control in capitalist society: a critical philosophy of legal order," pp. 181-202 in I. Taylor, P. Walton, and J. Young (eds.) Critical Criminology. Boston: Routledge & Kegan Paul.
SHERMAN, H. (1972) Radical Political Economy. New York: Basic Books.
WRIGHT, E. O. (1973) The Politics of Punishment. New York: Harper & Row.

John Braithwaite
Australian Institute of Criminology

4

PARADOXES OF CLASS BIAS
IN CRIMINAL JUSTICE

Class bias in criminal justice is defined broadly here as any systematic tendencies for legal institutions to impose more severe punishments on categories of persons lower in wealth, status, or power than on persons (or organizations) higher on any of those dimensions. The sources of class bias in the criminal justice system are many. Class bias can be manifested in a disproportionate tendency for working-class people who break the law to be subjected to surveillance rather than ignored, arrested rather than warned, prosecuted rather than have charges dropped, convicted rather than acquitted, subjected to a severe rather than a lenient sentence. The extent of such biases is the subject of considerable empirical dispute (Chiricos and Waldo, 1975; Greenberg, 1977a; Hagan, 1974; Lizotte, 1978; Liska and Tausig, 1979). Perhaps the most fundamental class bias, however, is the tendency for those types of crimes which are the prerogative of the powerful—white-collar crimes— to be given less attention by the criminal justice system than the other types of crimes (Hopkins, 1977; Reiman, 1979). This type of bias will be the focus of this chapter. White-collar crime will be defined here according to the conventional definition first articulated by Sutherland (1949: 2): "a crime committed by a person of respectability and high social status in the course of his [or her] occupation." Common or traditional crime in this chapter means all other offenses which are not white-collar.

The study will be structured around four propositions which lead to the following conclusion: To choose for a fundamentally more equitable criminal justice system in which the crimes of the powerful are no longer executed with impunity is to exacerbate certain other types of inequalities. It follows from the propositions that there can be no class justice in crime control policy, only choices between different forms of injustice.

Proposition 1: White-collar crime does more harm and is more common than traditional serious crime.

Harm is typically defined in one of two ways: objectively, according to the value of property stolen or the number of persons killed or injured, or subjectively, according to how serious members of the community say the offense is. On either measure, it is white-collar crime which causes greater harm. The now considerable evidence to this effect will not be reviewed here, as it has been detailed in a complementary article (Braithwaite, forthcoming). While it has long been accepted that the loss of property and injury to persons from white-collar offenses is greater than for common crimes, it is only in recent years that a formidable body of survey research evidence has accumulated showing that the public perceives many forms of white-collar crime as more serious, and deserving of more punishment, than most forms of common crime. No longer can it be asserted that the average citizen is unconcerned about and tolerant toward white-collar crime.

It is not only in terms of objective and subjective harm that white-collar offenses constitute a bigger problem than traditional crime; it is also in terms of the number of offenses and the number of offenders. The latter does not hold up if victimless crimes (drug use, consensual sexual offenses, etc.) and minor traffic violations are counted. This is why Proposition 1 used the words "serious crime," meaning crimes in which there are victims whose persons or property are threatened. The proposition that the number of white-collar offenses and offenders exceeds those for all other types of serious crimes can be supported by showing that certain offenses which constitute only a minor part of the white-collar crime problem are so common as to almost equal in number *all* the traditional offenses dealt with by the police.

A study of odometer fraud in Queensland, Australia found that over a third of vehicles randomly selected from used car lots had had their mileage readings turned back (Braithwaite, 1978). The sample in this study is not sufficient to permit us to assert confidently that this kind of fraud occurs for a third of the used cars sold in Queensland. Nevertheless, using a third as the best estimate available, there would be about 70,000 odometer frauds in Queensland each year. This is almost equal to the total of 80,181 offenses of all types (including victimless crimes, but excluding public order offenses such as drunkenness and vagrancy) reported to the Queensland police in the year of the study. For most odometer frauds there is a conspiracy involving more than one offender (Braithwaite, 1978).

Moving to a more respectable profession, Quinney (1963) found that 25 percent of pharmacists in Albany, New York had been found by government investigators to have violated prescription laws. Government surveys in two Australian jurisdictions have recently found 15 and 32 percent of gas pumps to be giving short-measure gas to motorists (Sunday Telegraph, February 3, 1980; Canberra Times, January 13, 1981). What, then, of serious crimes by large corporations, as opposed to the widespread dollars-and-cents frauds of gas station proprietors, used car dealers, and pharmacists? Few crimes could be more serious than bribing government health officials to entice them to allow a drug on the market which is banned in many other parts of the world. Yet in many countries this is common practice by transnational pharmaceutical companies (Braithwaite, 1982: chap. 2). Of the 20 largest American pharmaceutical companies, 19 have disclosed foreign bribes to the Securities and Exchange Commission. Looking at a wider range of offenses, Sutherland (1949) and Clinard et al. (1979) have been able to show that corporate crime is not a minority phenomenon among large American corporations, but that a majority of top companies violate the law on a fairly regular basis. All in all, this volume of offenses, combined with the inevitability of multiple offenders for each offense, is sufficient to invert conventional assessments of the class distribution of crime.

Proposition 2: Because of the volume of white-collar crime, consistent and equitable enforcement is not even remotely attainable. More punitive treatment of white-collar criminals implies that they will be treated less equitably.

Under this proposition I will attempt to show that with white-collar crime there is little hope of even approximating the principle that offenders who have committed the same offense should be punished equally severely. Further, it will be concluded that any attempt to step up the prosecution of white-collar criminals will worsen the inequities of treatment among white-collar criminals. By attempting to redress the imbalance of treatment between white-collar criminals as a class and common criminals as a class, we widen the sentencing disparities within the class of white-collar criminals. To develop this argument, let us first return to some concrete examples.

Only 40 prosecutions of gas station proprietors followed from the aforementioned survey by the New South Wales Department of Consumer Affairs (Sunday Telegraph, February 3, 1980). Some particularly bad cases were singled out for the purpose of achieving deterrence. Meting out "just deserts" to all the offenders would have tied up more of the agency's resources than it could afford. Similarly, continually having a quarter of the pharmacists or of the auto dealers in a jurisdiction being processed for prosecution would bankrupt the wealthiest of governments. The impossibility of consistent and equitable enforcement becomes more profound with more serious types of cases, because these are the ones which are most complex and therefore most costly at both the investigation and litigation stages.

Writers who in other areas have been attracted to just deserts as a basis for criminal sentencing have concluded that white-collar crime is one area where it is undesirable to attempt consistently to administer just deserts. Norval Morris (1974: 79), who advocates that desert set an upper limit on sanctions, says of tax violations: "Not every tax felon need be imprisoned, only a number sufficient to keep the law's promises and to encourage the rest of us to honesty in our tax returns."

It is for white-collar crimes against the person, the very crimes which the community feels deserve most punishment (Scott and Al-Thakeb, 1977; Cullen et al., 1980; Schrager and Short, 1980; Wolfgang, 1980), that the case for selective enforcement is strongest. This is because the offense so often poses a continuing danger to the community. Just deserts must at times be sacrificed for protection of the public. Regulatory agencies often resist the urge to prosecute guilty parties when the cooperation of those parties is needed to safeguard the public health. If a drug company has criminally negligent quality control procedures that are putting the community at risk, an injunction to close down the plant followed by a criminal prosecution can set company lawyers to work on very effective delaying tactics (see Green, 1978). Justice delayed is profits retained. The public interest will often be better served by an approach to the company offering immunity from prosecution if it will cooperate in a package of measures, which might include a voluntary recall of impure drugs from the market, dismissal of certain irresponsible quality control staff, revision of standard operating procedures to improve product quality, and compensation to victims of the impure drugs. Such negotiated settlements foster deterrence, more so than a paltry fine which might be handed down by a court. But more important, they achieve deterrence while minimizing the risk to consumers. A voluntary recall of drugs already on the market is almost invariably more rapid and efficient (in the sense of maximizing the proportion of the batch that is located) than a court-ordered seizure (Hutt, 1973: 177). Only the company knows where all of its product has gone. A seizure that is resisted by the company faces considerable practical difficulties.

A classic illustration of the dilemmas in choosing between retribution against alleged white-collar criminals and the wider public interest was the aftermath of the thalidomide drug disaster (Knightley et al., 1979: 122-136). Nine executives of Chemie Grünenthal, the manufacturer of thalidomide, were indicted in Germany on charges of intent to commit bodily harm and involuntary manslaughter. After the complex legal proceedings had dragged on for five years, including over two years in court, the charges were dropped as part of a deal in which Grünenthal agreed to pay $31 million in compensation to the German thalidomide children. The press cried "justice for sale!" But the German government had to consider the ongoing misery of the thalidomide families who up to that point had struggled for nine years rearing their deformed and limbless children without any financial assistance. Would retribution against Grünenthal and its executives have justified perhaps another nine years of limbo and deprivation for the victims?

There are many reasons against prosecuting even some violations that endanger human life. Government safety inspectors have an educative role that is more important than their enforcement role. Many unsafe practices are not covered by the law. The inspector must build up a store of goodwill with companies in order to persuade them to change unsafe practices, to improve quality assurance systems, when such changes are not really required by law (Blau, 1955: 165-178). One very effective way for inspectors to generate the goodwill necessary to persuade companies to improve their standard operating procedures is to "give a second chance" to company officers who have broken the law. Obversely, prosecuting offenses which were unintentional can foster resentment and dissipate motivation to improve. Another reason for inconsistent enforcement of the law is that it is usually good inspectorial practice not to recommend a prosecution when the company comes forward and admits the violation, even in many circumstances where the offense is serious. This is because the government must encourage companies to come forward with their safety problems so that they can assist in finding solutions and warn the public of the danger.

Although there are many more compelling reasons for not consistently prosecuting white-collar offenders, cost is undoubtedly the most influential reason in practice. Philip Schrag's (1971) gripping account of what happened when he took over the enforcement division of the New York City Department of Consumer Affairs underlines the inevitability of a retreat from commitment to consistent and equitable enforcement of the law when dealing with white-collar crime. When Schrag began the job he adopted a prosecutorial stance. But in response to a variety of frustrations, especially the use of delaying tactics by company lawyers, a "direct action" model was eventually substituted for the "judicial" model. Nonlitigious methods of achieving restitution, deterrence, and incapacitation were increasingly used. These included threats and use of adverse publicity, revocation of license, writing directly to consumers to warn them of company practices, and exerting pressure on reputable financial institutions and suppliers to withdraw support for the targeted company.

Whether we approve the retreat from the justice model with white-collar crime or not, it must be conceded that, given the clumsy legal system we have inherited, the public gets most of its protection from extralegal muscle-flexing by regulators. We might shudder at the cavalier disregard of due process by the inspector who says, "Fix that up or I'll be back once a month looking for things to nab you on." But to the extent that white-collar crime is prevented in modern societies, that is the most important kind of way it happens. Moreover, I suspect that most companies would prefer to live with a little of such standover every now and then than with the legal costs of a more litigious relationship with government agencies.

At the same time, most regulatory agencies are cognizant of the habit-forming value of law. Most individuals obey the law because they think it immoral to disobey. One of the reasons they think it immoral is that they sometimes see society punish other people for disobeying. A degree of formal and public punishment is also necessary to maintain general deterrence. These ends can be achieved by white-collar crime enforcement policies in which only occasional offenders are made an example of. The offenders chosen are usually those for whom none of the aforementioned arguments against prosecution apply. They are chosen not because they are the most "deserving" of punishment but because their case would be less costly than others, because their cooperation is not required to retrieve dangerous drugs from the market, and so on.

The Food and Drug Administration, for example, settles for a warning rather than prosecution in over 90 percent of first offenses reported by its inspectors. Such a policy is plainly contrary to the principle that those who have committed the same offense should be punished equally severely. A small minority of first offenders is victimized on grounds that have little to do with justice. One solution is to enact a rule forbidding prosecution for *any* first offender. This, however, would sacrifice crime prevention for equity and consistency. A rule that no offender will be prosecuted unless it has been previously warned reduces incentives for law observance among firms that have not yet been warned (Kriesberg, 1976: 113).

Food and drug lawyers, in fact, are forever voicing concern about the inconsistency of selective prosecution, advocating rulemaking to constrain the administrative discretion that makes possible inequitable treatment of food and drug offenders. These champions of equity, however, do not stop to consider the inequity between food and drug versus other types of offenders. The most fundamental inequity in criminal justice systems is that serious white-collar crimes are carried off with impunity while prisons bulge with minor working-class criminals. Given the unworkability of consistent enforcement of white-collar crime, the only route to consistency is to cease the victimization of the few. Yet the latter equity could only be achieved at the expense of further exacerbating the inequality between the treatment of white-collar criminals as a class and common criminals as a class. Petty disparities between offenders of the same type are narrowed only to widen more fundamental structural disparities between white-collar and traditional offenders. This is a feature of efforts to reduce any kind of petty inequality that ignore global inequality. For example, equalizing income disparities among doctors by raising the remuneration of GPs to that of specialists achieves petty equality among doctors. However, it also increases societal inequality by further widening the gap between doctors as a class and the rest of the population.

When the resident of an affluent suburb is convicted of tax evasion, many neighbors are secretly struck by the injustice of this person being singled out. Perhaps not many of them are impressed, however, by the injustice of the way the law treats their suburb as a whole compared with some other neighborhoods in the city.

For all types of white-collar crime, only a tiny minority of known offenders is prosecuted. Many areas of common crime, in contrast, see a situation where the majority of apprehended known offenders are prosecuted, even if for a different offense in a plea bargain. Certainly apprehending common criminals is difficult, but once caught, they are generally convicted. Areas of common crime where this is not true include petty offenses regarded as not serious enough to tie up over-burdened courts. The relevant comparison here, however, is between serious white-collar crime and serious common crime. With the former we see a situation where a tiny minority of known and apprehended offenders is prosecuted. As a consequence, the easiest way to achieve more equity (in fact, the only way) is to stop victimizing the few. With serious common crimes, where majority prosecutions of known and apprehended offenders are more likely, the shortest route to equity is to prosecute the minority of guilty persons who at present have their charges dropped. Hence, with white-collar crime the least radical depar-ture from existing practice to achieve equity would be to prosecute *no* suspects; with serious common crime the least radical change would be to prosecute *all* suspects. Within both classes, policies to increase the proportion of apprehended offenders who receive the same treatment (prosecution with common criminals, nonprosecution with white-collar criminals) will widen interclass differences.

Moreover, even if it is not true that a majority of apprehended offenders are prosecuted for most serious common crimes (consider rape, for example), the argument about the white-collar crime side of the equation still applies. Irrespective of what policies we adopt with respect to traditional crime, if 90 percent of known white-collar offenders of a particular type are currently set free, then increasing this figure toward 100 percent will increase the consistency with which we treat those white-collar offenders. Such a policy will also widen the disparity between white-collar and common offenders so long as changes in policies toward common crime are not so dramatic to have reversed the assumption that common criminals are punished more than white-collar criminals.

A public policy choice is therefore called for. Which is more important —individual inequalities among white-collar criminals who have com-mitted the same offense, or structural inequality between white-collar offenders as a class and traditional criminals as a class? Radicals will opt for the latter as more important because it is a form of inequality based on power. The former, in contrast, is a form of inequality based more on chance. Working-class offenders are treated more harshly than white-collar criminals because they have less power; they do not command the resources to employ top lawyers; they engage in simple crimes for which guilt is easily proven because they do not have the capital for the finan-cial manipulations which provide a safe haven of complexity. In contrast, those white-collar offenders who are prosecuted are victimized not because they have less power than other white-collar offenders but in considerable measure because they are plain unlucky. Perhaps they were unlucky because their impure batch of drugs caused visible symptoms in patients rather than invisible symptoms, because the government was able to obtain records which they neglected to shred, or because their case was not so complex as to be beyond the comprehension of a jury.

It can be argued that inequality based on chance should be of less concern to those who form public policy than inequality based on power. We are forever being victims of chance inequality. Some of us go through life without breaking a bone in our body while others are always falling down stairs. Nothing can or should be done about the kind of inequality that leaves some of us in plaster while others play golf. Public policy does not concern itself with inequality based on chance alone because it is assumed that while misfortune will frown on us with respect to some chance inequalities, good luck will smile on us with others. Not so with inequality based on power. The fact that one is a victim because of powerlessness increases the probability that one will be a victim in many other kinds of ways. Powerlessness begets victimization begets powerlessness begets more victimization. This is what is meant by "self-perpetuating poverty" or "cycles of disadvantage" (Rutter and Madge, 1976). Public policy therefore rightly has a greater concern with rooting out structural inequality based on power in all its insidious forms than with removing inequality based on chance. This is why inequality among white-collar offenders should be of less concern than inequality between white-collar offenders as a class and traditional criminals as a class. It is why we should be prepared to accept increased prosecution of white-collar criminals even though those who face prosecution will justly feel that they have been arbitrarily selected from a large pool of unpunished white-collar criminals.

In developing this argument, the extent to which inequality among white-collar offenders is based on chance has been overstated. Governments are less inclined to prosecute large pharmaceutical companies than small ones (Braithwaite, 1982); similarly, the Internal Revenue Service devotes only 2.5 percent of its investigation time to corporations with over $250 million in assets (Saxon, 1980: 42). Moreover, we will see later that when individuals are brought to account for organizational crimes, they are often junior scapegoats who carry the blame for more senior criminals. It remains true, nevertheless, that the structural inequality between the way white-collar and traditional criminals are treated has more to do with power than the inequality between the way prosecuted and nonprosecuted white-collar criminals are treated.

Proposition 3: White-collar criminals can use their power:

    (a) to prevent prosecution,
    (b) to displace blame downward in the class structure,
    (c) to place blame on the organization rather than on powerful individuals within it.

(a) *To prevent prosecution.* White-collar criminals occasionally prevent their prosecution through the sheer exercise of political muscle. Politicians afraid of losing campaign contributions or patronage from powerful individuals have been known to influence prosecutors (Clinard and Yeager, 1980: 143-145). A more important deterrent to prosecution, however, is the generalized reluctance of conservative bureaucrats to bait powerful actors who can bite back and who are able to hire more competent lawyers than the government is willing to pay for. These competent lawyers, in turn, can further push up the cost disincentives of prosecution by using delaying tactics (Green, 1978).

Much has been written about how the complexity of white-collar crimes makes conviction difficult (Edelhertz, 1970; Harvard Law Review, 1979; Stone, 1975). In part, this complexity is inherent in offenses that are embedded in complex financial transactions or convoluted organizational realities or that involve difficult scientific questions. Equally, however, the complexity which makes conviction forlorn is contrived by the white collar criminal. The books of account are confusing because the criminal wants them that way. What could be a simple transaction between A and B is intentionally concealed by a round robin or daisy chain arrangement through a series of intermediary transactions.

The case is similar with organizational complexity. Every individual in a large organization can present a different version of what company policy was, and individual corporate actors can blame others for their own actions (x says he was following y's instructions, y says that x misunderstood instructions she had passed down from z, ad infinitum). So how can either company policy or any individual company employee be guilty? Even if this is not the reality, it is difficult for the prosecution to prove otherwise. Many corporations present to the outside world a picture of diffused accountability for law observance while ensuring that lines of accountability are in fact clearly defined for internal law compliance purposes. Companies have two kinds of records: those designed to allocate guilt (for internal purposes) and those for obscuring guilt (for presentation to the outside world, see Braithwaite, 1982).

(b) *To displace blame downward in the class structure.* White-collar criminals do not normally set out with the purpose of committing a crime in the way a bank robber does. Rather, the white-collar criminal wishes to achieve certain goals related to his or her occupation (increasing profits, reaching a production target, election to office) and violation of the law is something that happens in the course of pursuing a means to the goal. It is not difficult for powerful actors to structure their affairs so that all of the pressures to break the law surface at lower levels of their own organization, or in another subordinate organization. Hence, the American executive who wants to sell products to Middle Eastern governments hires an agent to do the negotiation. The agent is paid an enormous fee, which is sufficient to cover bribes to government officials (Jacoby et al., 1977; Kennedy and Simon, 1978). The drug company, which would not dream of putting pressure on its own scientists to compromise their standards of integrity, will give a toxicological testing job on a new drug to an outside laboratory known for its sloppy standards. The contract laboratory maintains its popularity with the pharmaceutical giant by telling it what it wants to hear about the safety of the drug, even if that involves fudging data (Braithwaite, 1982: chap. 3). The reputable chemical corporation can contract out disposal of toxic materials to a waste disposal company, which, being controlled by organized crime, is not particularly fussy about environmental protection laws (Raab, 1980).

In these situations, the superordinate organization cuts costs by having the subordinate organization do the job to standards that would be unconscionable in-house. The advantages of white-collar crime are attained without anyone in the dominant organization being a white-collar criminal. This phenomenon has been most systematically demonstrated in the automobile industry. Leonard and Weber (1970) showed how the oligopolistic control over the supply of new cars by the Big Three in the 1960s allowed them to impose sales quotas on their franchised dealers, who were then forced to turn to consumer fraud in order to move their cars in sufficient volume to stay afloat. General Motors does not perpetuate the frauds which include "accessories not ordered but 'forced' on buyers, used cars sold for new, engines switched in cars, excessive finance charges, automotive repair overcharges, 'fake' repair diagnoses" (Leonard and Weber, 1970: 415-416). However, General

Motors is, in Taft's (1966) terms, a "dangerous person" who sets economic conditions that have the effect of driving subordinates into crime. Farberman (1975: 456), in a participant-observation study of automotive dealers, confirmed Leonard and Weber's conclusion:

> In sum, a limited number of oligopolistic manufacturers who sit at the pinnacle of an economically concentrated industry can establish economic policy which creates a market structure that causes lower level dependent industry participants to engage in patterns of illegal activity.

Denzin (1977) has found similar criminogenic market pressures at work in the liquor industry (see also Needleman and Needleman, 1979). These pressures on responsibility for illegality percolate downward within organizations as well as between them. While used car sales managers are put under enormous pressure by quotas imposed on them by the distributor, these pressures are passed on to salespersons who, in turn, are set their quotas by the sales managers. If salespersons do not meet the quota, they are dismissed. Hence, within used car firms, it is often the salesperson who comes to the manager pleading for approval (or a blind eye) for the turning back of odometers (Braithwaite, 1978). If you set up a cutthroat system, some throats are going to get cut.

The classic illustration of the passing of blame downward in the class structure is with mining. A common strategy of mine owners is to put workers on piece rates based on the amount of coal or asbestos extracted in a given day. Such a strategy often produces the situation of miners wanting to go into workings that are unsafe, or even doing so against the counsel of management (Scott, 1974: 220).

Blame is not always passed all the way down to blue-collar workers. The chief executive officers of some (at least two) transnational pharmaceutical companies have "vice-presidents responsible for going to jail" (Braithwaite, 1982). Lines of accountability are drawn in the organization so that if someone's head must go on the chopping block, it will be that of the vice-president responsible for going to jail. This person takes the (very slight) risk in return for promotion to vice-president, and undoubtedly a period of faithful performance in the role would be rewarded by a sideways shift to a safe vice-presidency. A more mundane example is the use of dummy directors by New South Wales transport companies which evade road maintenance tax. The executive director of the Long Distance Road Transport Association has said of these directors who are paid to go to jail: "I've heard of a few cases in which the dummy directors were alcoholics who were quite happy to dry out in jail for a few weeks."

Concomitant with the passing of blame downward is a need to ensure that the taint of knowledge about the nefarious activities of more junior people does not bounce back upward. Gross (1978: 203) has explained the importance of screening "bad news" about law breaking from those at the top:

> A job of the lawyers is often to prevent such information from reaching the top officers so as to protect them from the taint of knowledge should the company later end up in court. One of the reasons former President Nixon got into such trouble was that those near him did not feel such solicitude but, from self-protective motives presumably, made sure he did know every detail of the illegal activities that were going on.

The heavy electrical equipment price-fixing conspiracy of the 1950s demonstrated various communication blockages orchestrated from above. Senior managers intentionally ruptured line reporting to prevent low-level employees from passing up their concern over illegalities.

> Even when subordinates had sought to protest orders they considered questionable, they found themselves checked by the linear structure of authority, which effectively denied them any means by which to appeal. For example, one almost Kafkaesque ploy utilized to prevent an appeal by a subordinate was to have a person substantially above the level of his immediate superior ask him to engage in the questionable practice. The immediate superior would then be told not to supervise the activities of the subordinate in the given area. Thus, both the subordinate and the supervisor would be left in the dark regarding the level of authority from which the order had come, to whom an appeal might lie, and whether they would violate company policy by even discussing the matter between themselves. By in effect removing the subject employee from his normal organizational terrain, this stratagem effectively structured an information blockage into the corporate communication system. Interestingly, there are striking similarities between such an organizational pattern and the manner in which control over corporate slush funds deliberately was given to low-level employees, whose activities then were carefully exempted from the supervision of their immediate superiors [Coffee, 1977: 1133].

Although the downward pressure on responsibility for law breaking is a ubiquitous phenomenon, the extent to which it results from conscious manipulation by those at the top is variable. In many corporations the president might not be aware that his loyal henchman, the executive vice-president, has set up a system to protect both of them through the expedient of nominating junior scapegoats. Middle managers might not have to be told to protect top management from the taint of knowledge. They may perceive their job as achieving the goals set them without worrying top management with the sordid details of how they do it. In any case, middle managers score more points by pretending that they have achieved their goals legally (without exposing the corporation to risk) through sheer managerial competence. Were the president to know the details, he might genuinely be shocked.

This reality renders comprehensible a fascinating finding from a national sample survey of 236 managers (Carrol, 1975, 1978). Top managers split equally on the proposition: "Managers today feel under pressure to compromise personal standards to achieve company goals." In contrast, 65 percent of the middle managers and 85 percent of the lower managers agreed with it. Cressey and Moore (1980: 48) have reported on surveys within the Uniroyal and Pitney Bowes corporations which reached the same conclusion. At Pitney Bowes, 25 percent of persons earning over $30,000 agreed that they had to compromise personal standards to achieve company goals compared to 59 percent of those earning under $30,000. The interpretation that would follow from the analysis in this section is that middle and lower managers *feel* under greater pressure to compromise personal standards because they *are* under greater pressure to do so (see also Getschow, 1979).

The increasingly transnational nature of business means that the possibilities for those at the top of the organization to distance themselves from the dirty work become more and more profound.

> Headquarters may insist that their subsidiaries meet certain profit (or other) goals, while at the same time making it clear that headquarters can hardly be intimately acquainted with the laws of foreign countries. Hence, under the guise of local autonomy (which may be hailed as throwing off the shackles of colonialism by local enthusiasts), the subsidiary may be forced to engage in crime for which *they will be held responsible by their governments*. Meanwhile, headquarters (in New York, Tokyo, or Rotterdam), while hardly pleased with the result (loss of income), nevertheless escapes criminal prosecution [Gross, 1978: 209].

(c) *To place blame on the organization rather than on powerful individuals within it.* Juries are notoriously reluctant to convict individual executives even in situations where the conviction of the corporation would seem to imply that there must have been guilty individuals as well (Harvard Law Review, 1979: 1248-1249). Allocating individual guilt is extremely difficult if all corporate actors are determined to propagate a smokescreen of diffused accountability. Each individual who might be called to account can be instructed to point the finger at someone else whose orders they were following, and they in turn can be told to point the finger at yet another person, or to say that their instructions were misunderstood. With the corporation of all involved, the most palpable instances of individual guilt can be quite readily beat up into a My Lai syndrome. Equally, a Lieutenant Calley can often be scapegoated for the most blatant instances of top management guilt.

Organizations do not normally want to sacrifice a Lieutenant Calley who might be so aggrieved by his employer as to be willing to help the authorities pierce the smokescreen of diffused responsibility. Moreover, employers are usually genuinely concerned to protect their faithful employees from victimization. Hence, blaming the organization is often a more attractive strategy than blaming a scapegoat. No one wants to see blood spilled, and organizations which are hurt do not bleed in the way individuals do. While a guilty individual is at risk of imprisonment, a guilty corporation cannot go to jail—at worst it might get a heavy fine, the costs of which can be spread among consumers, shareholders and employers without hurting anyone perceptibly.

> *Proposition 4: Because of this power of white-collar criminals, prosecutors have little option but to adopt policies that result in convicted white-collar criminals being treated more leniently than common criminals.*

Placing blame on the organization is a strategy that usually works because the prosecutor is dealing with an offense to which the only witnesses are individuals within the organization who are themselves implicated in the offense. The only way the "blaming the organization" strategy can be foiled is by winning insiders to testify as to who did issue critical instructions and approvals. Similarly, the strategy of sacrificing junior scapegoats can only be foiled by "flipping" a witness (usually the scapegoat). If the scapegoat has been or is being in some way rewarded by the organization for taking the rap, then the prosecutor can only entice him to turn on the organization with a bigger reward. As Ogren (1973: 974) remarked: "It is no surprise that government witnesses to many fraud cases include the sleazy, the corrupt and the guilty who were not indicted, a demonstration of the price the government must pay to prosecute its prime targets." Hagan and Burnstein (1979: 472) point out that judges cooperate in helping prosecutors make their payoff to insiders who come across. One assistant U.S. attorney in their study remarked: "I would say most judges understand that in order to expose official corruption you do have to give some concessions to people who are involved. Again, because only those people who are involved know and can testify about it."

The white-collar crime prosecutor can therefore adopt a strategy counterbalancing the forces that push blame downward in the organizational hierarchy. Favorable plea bargains or immunity can be offered to A to establish a case against his superior, B. B having been placed in the breach, she can be flipped to testify against her superior, C, and so on up the organization. Dilemmas are confronted in such wheeling and dealing. Should one grant immunity to a middle manager who is the single most blameworthy individual in the organization in order to have him testify against several of his superiors, who each may be someone less blameworthy than he? While the negotiation and guesswork would seem to sacrifice fairness terribly, it does hew a rough justice by pitting one form of unfairness which pushes up the class structure against another which pushes down. The criminal justice system can choose the reactive path of fairly treating people who have been unfairly handed to it as scapegoats, or it can conclude that the more important injustice is that which always hooks the small fish while the big ones get away. For the sake of righting this structural injustice, it might be deemed justifiable to tolerate inconsistent treatment of equally guilty individuals involved in the same crime.

If a prosecutor's office wants to bring many white-collar criminals to justice, especially the more powerful ones among them, it has no choice but to offer immunity, favorable plea bargains, and prospects of leniency in sentencing to flip guilty insiders. The more this proactive dealing is done, the larger grow the numbers of white-collar criminals who are treated leniently on the conviction. Paradoxically, then, the gap widens between the severity of the sanctions handed out to white-collar criminals as a class compared to traditional criminals as a class. Hagan et al. (1980) have shown empirically that this may be exactly what happens. Comparing 10 federal district attorney offices, they found that the most proactive office, the one that brought most white-collar criminals to justice, was also the office that achieved the most lenient average sentences for white-collar criminals. The study showed, then, that "there may be an inverse relationship between the volume of white-collar prosecutions and the severity with which they are sentenced" (Hagan et al., 1980: 802).

There is another reason for the paradox that more lenient treatment of convicted white-collar criminals will be associated with more white-collar criminals being convicted. It was argued earlier that proving guilt in complex white-collar crimes is more difficult than with traditional crimes. One of the few ways of bringing more white-collar criminals to justice is to strip white-collar criminals, especially corporate criminals, of some of the due process protections which make conviction so extraordinarily difficult. Reasonable arguments can be advanced that many due process protections, which were enacted historically to protect powerless individuals from abuse of the superior power of the state, should not be relevant to organizations that themselves approach or exceed the state in power. Certainly they typically surpass the state in their capacity to hire expensive legal talent. The U.S. Supreme Court has long denied corporations the privilege against self-incrimination (Hale v. Henkel, 201 U.S. 43, 75 [1906]). The Court has accepted that publicly traded companies "can claim no equality with individuals in the enjoyment of a right to privacy." (U.S. v. Morton Salt Co., 338 U.S. 632 [1950]). Perhaps proof "beyond reasonable doubt" should be replaced by proof "on the balance of probabilities" in many complex types of white-collar cases where the former is an impossible burden. In environmental cases involving scientific disputes over whether company policy X caused environmental impact Y, proof beyond reasonable doubt is logically impossible given the probabilistic nature of science.

Any decision to jettison due process protections, no matter how reasonably based, must be balanced against the rights of the suspect. We tolerate the fact that we have almost no due process protections when found guilty of a parking offense largely because the penalties are not very severe. Packer (1968: 131) argued that the stigma and loss of liberty of imprisonment is the oppressive measure which sets apart the need for due process protections. The full paraphernalia of traditional procedural protections certainly should be available when there is any possibility of imprisonment. When lesser penalties such as fines are involved, American courts have been willing to relax the guarantees of the Sixth Amendment, the protection against double jeopardy and the requirement of proof beyond reasonable doubt (Harvard Law Review, 1979: 1306-1307). This makes a tempting case for removing imprisonment provisions from many white-collar crime statutes. The apparent tradeoff of less severity for more certainty is hardly a tradeoff at all, given the demonstrated unwillingness of courts to send senior executives to prison.

Whether the criminal justice system *should* trade off severity for more convictions, this is in fact what it does. When OSHA lawyers are confronted with a choice between recommending to the Justice Department a civil prosecution (with less onerous burdens of proof) which would attract only a fine and a criminal prosecution, in all but a handful of cases in the history of the act they have opted for the civil route (Levin, 1977). The same is true of antitrust enforcement (Posner, 1976: 25; Saxon, 1980: 55), the enforcement of the Food, Drug and Cosmetic Act (Braithwaite, 1982), and the enforcement activities of the Securities and Exchange Commission (Reisman, 1979).

While the critics of prosecutors who take the easier civil route are many (Bequai, 1976; Green et al., 1972; Reisman, 1979), the unarguable fact is that such a choice generates more deterrence for the severely limited prosecutorial dollar. A considerable increase in the number of convictions is achieved at the expense of only moderate reductions in the average severity of sentence that would result under the criminal route. As with the earlier choices, however, the more efficient enforcement of the law against white-collar criminals is achieved at the expense of widening the disparity between the punishments given to convicted white-collar criminals and those exacted against common criminals.

CONCLUSION

It has been argued that the most fundamental inequality in our criminal justice system is that the crimes of the powerful are both the most harmful and the least sanctioned, while the powerless are sanctioned often and severely. A just society would have many more white-collar criminals in prison than common criminals. Yet when prosecutors attempt to redress this injustice, they worsen other injustices: namely that of unequal treatment of offenders who have committed the same offense and that of convicted common criminals attracting heavier average sentences than convicted white-collar criminals whose offenses are equally serious.

Because justice is inevitably balanced against other important goals when dealing with white-collar crime—ensuring the safety of the public, protecting the jobs of innocent employees, keeping the wheels of industry turning, restraining the costs of administering justice within the capacity of taxpayers—any attempt to tip back the scales of injustice can only be achieved by selective prosecution of white-collar criminals. Such selectivity conflicts with the important equitable principle that offenders who have committed the same crime should be similarly punished.

The choice here is not a noble one. Some would contend that the only proper course is to strive to prosecute the powerful nonselectively, whatever the costs. Bankrupting a society by putting a substantial proportion of its pharmacists, doctors, and business executives behind bars, sacrificing the suffering of consumers for the sake of litigated justice, are hardly noble choices. More important, they are choices that could never be made, given what we know about how states struggle against fiscal crisis (O'Connor, 1973). More intensive, yet selective, enforcement of white-collar crime, in turn, can be painted as the best policy, but never as a noble one. It is ignoble in retreating from the just principle of equal treatment of offenders who have done equal wrongs, and in reaching that position through yielding meekly to the bargaining power of the white-collar criminals who remain unpunished. It is a policy which explicitly eschews moving toward a position where all offenders of a given type are treated the same. Instead we make a small minority shoulder the guilt of the unpunished majority of white-collar criminals.

The second conclusion is that redressing the balance by bringing more white-collar criminals to justice will widen the disparity between the average punishment administered to convicted white-collar and traditional criminals. This is because the number of fish caught is a function of how many others are promised leniency (Hagan et al., 1980). Moreover, the size of the catch can be increased by proceeding under statutes that offer fewer due process protections but less punitive sanctions.

Again, public policy must choose which is the lesser of the two evils. The status quo wherein white-collar criminals are seldom brought to justice is surely the greater evil. Better to have a large increase in the number punished even if the quantum of punishment pales beside that bestowed on common criminals. We can only hope that as more white-collar criminals are convicted but sentenced more leniently than working-class criminals who have done lesser harm, demands will increase for less severe treatment of the underclasses who fill our prisons. Such demands will only become more focused, however, when white-collar criminals begin to be brought to justice in numbers.

Paradoxically, if we approach equity between white-collar and common criminals from the other end, by treating common criminals more leniently, we have come full circle. As some common criminals (who previously might have been given 10 years) benefit from the new leniency, inequity grows between them and offenders who are still serving their 10 years for the same kind of offense. As some common criminals are not punished because the victim is willing to agree to restitution, injustice is exacerbated for those criminals whose victims are not so cooperative. Nevertheless, while the shift toward leniency exacerbates injustices within the class of common criminals, inequality of treatment between the classes of common and white-collar criminals is attenuated.

This returns us to the question of which is more important—intraclass or interclass inequality? Again, the kind of injustice which causes some common criminals to be punished more heavily than others is based more on luck (drawing a lenient judge, a forgiving victim), whereas the injustice of punishing common criminals more harshly than white-collar criminals is based more on power. As I argued earlier, for good reason public policy is less concerned about inequality based on chance than with rooting out self-perpetuating structural forms of inequality.

These arguments are made the more telling by the fact that there is also an institutional dimension to the tendency for blame to be passed downward in the class structure. The rising concern over white-collar crime which came in the wake of Watergate was a concern over abuses by those with power (the Nixons, ITTs, and Lockheeds). Yet this concern has been captured by the powerful and turned to their interests. Today the predominant push against white-collar crime is to protect large organizations (corporations and governments) from crimes against them by employees, welfare claimants, and other less powerful actors. Computer crime has been made the type of white-collar crime which grips the public imagination—the malevolent mathematical genius defrauding the large corporation. The effect of widespread use of public money to catch computer criminals is, in aggregate, to redistribute wealth from the average taxpayer to the large organizations which are saved from computer crime victimization. What of the powerless individuals who cannot afford to own computers? Why, they have become the white-collar criminals. Hence, in Hagan et al.'s (1980) empirical study of white-collar offenders (in which the latter were defined operationally as individuals convicted of fraud, bribery, conspiracy to defraud, embezzlement, etc.) most white-collar criminals would seem to have had blue-collars! More precisely, 74 percent of the "white-collar criminals" earned less than $13,776 a year in deflated dollars, and 63 percent of them had only a high school education or less.

The institutional pressures to pass blame for our social problems downward in the class structure are all-pervasive. Economic crisis, for example, is more likely to be explained by lazy welfare cheats than by incompetent capitalists. The criminal justice system is central to this process. There is a great deal of evidence that during economic crisis, when unemployment increases, the criminal justice system becomes more punitive and prison populations swell with lower-class criminals (Box and Hale, 1982; Braithwaite, 1980; Greenberg, 1977b; Jankovic, 1977; Quinney, 1977; Yeager, 1979). Underclasses provide individual scapegoats for our collective failures. Policies that attempt to reverse the normal pressures to pass blame downward therefore have a more transcendental virtue than simply the restoration of justice. They are part of a struggle against a pervasive mystification that victimizes the poor in an infinite variety of ways.

Finally, there is the utilitarian rationale for stepping up prosecution of white-collar criminals even in the face of the other inequalities thereby exacerbated. Because the harm from white-collar crime is so much greater than that of traditional crime, and because the former is more preventable than the latter (Braithwaite and Geis, 1982), in the compromise between utilitarian and justice goals the white-collar crime emphasis should shift somewhat toward utilitarianism. There is evidence to suggest that the coal mine fatality rate today is less than a quarter of its level of 40 years ago because of the enforcement activities of the Bureau of Mines (Lewis-Beck and Alford, 1980). Many rivers that were once polluted are now relatively clean thanks to the Environmental Protection Agency. Modest consumer product safety enforcement in recent years has produced a 40 percent drop in ingestion of poisons by children, a halving of crib deaths of babies, and virtual elimination of children's sleepwear as a cause of flameburn injuries (Costle, 1979). It might be that we are prepared to tolerate some injustice to achieve these kinds of goals.

For deterrence to work, sanctions do not have to be consistently applied to all offenders. Selective enforcement need be sufficient only to make deterrent threats credible. In most areas of white-collar crime, however, enforcement falls short of credibility. Deterrence demands more convictions. Are we willing to shy away from this by invoking the selective injustice that will inexorably follow from it? A public policy choice cannot be avoided between the injustice of selectivity and the structural injustice that blinks at the abuses of the rich while bludgeoning those of the poor.

REFERENCES

BEQUAI, A. (1976) "Why the SEC's enforcer is in over his head." Business Week (October 11): 70.

BLAU, P. (1955) The Dynamics of Bureaucracy. Chicago: Univ. of Chicago Press.

BOX, S. and HALE, C. (1982) "Unemployment, crime and imprisonment," in National Deviancy Conference, Class and Social Justice. London: Hutchinson.

BRAITHWAITE, J. (1982) Corporate Crime in the Pharmaceutical Industry. London: Routledge & Kegan Paul.

—————— (1980) "The political economy of punishment," pp. 192-208 in E. L. Wheelwright and K. Buckley (eds.) Essays in the Political Economy of Australian Capitalism, Volume 4. Sydney: ANZ Books.

—————— (1978) "An exploratory study of used car fraud," pp. 101-122 in P. R. Wilson and J. Braithwaite (eds.) Two Faces of Deviance: Crimes of the Powerless and Powerful. Brisbane: Univ. of Queensland Press.

—————— (forthcoming) "Challenging just deserts: the sentencing of white-collar criminals." J. of Criminal Law and Criminology.

—————— and G. GEIS (1982) "On theory and action for corporate crime control." Crime and Delinquency.

CARROL, A. B. (1978) "Business ethics and the management hierarchy." National Forum 18: 37-40.

—————— (1975) "Management ethics: a post-Watergate view." Business Horizons (April) 75-80.

CHIRICOS, T. G. and G. P. WALDO (1975) "Socioeconomic status and criminal sentencing: an empirical assessment of a conflict proposition." Amer. Soc. Rev. 40: 753-772.

CLINARD, M. B. and P. C. YEAGER (1980) Corporate Crime. New York: Free Press.

—————— J. BRISSETTE, D. PETRASHEK, and E. HARRIES (1979) Illegal Corporate Behavior. Washington DC: Law Enforcement Assistance Administration.

COFFEE, J. C., Jr. (1977) "Beyond the shut-eyed sentry: toward a theoretical view of corporate misconduct and an effective legal response." Virginia Law Rev. 63: 1099-1278.

CONKLIN, J. E. (1977) Illegal But Not Criminal: Business Crime in America. Englewood Cliffs, NJ: Prentice-Hall.

COSTLE, D. M. (1979) "Innovative regulation." Economic Impact 28: 8-14.

CRESSEY, D. R. and C. A. MOORE (1980) Corporation Codes of Ethical Conduct. New York: Peat, Marwick and Mitchell Foundation.

CULLEN, F. T., B. G. LINK, and C. W. POLANZI (1980) "The seriousness of crime revisited: have attitudes toward white-collar crime changed?" Presented at the American Society of Criminology annual meeting, San Francisco.

DENZIN, N. K. (1977) "Notes on the criminogenic hypothesis: a case study of the American liquor industry." Amer. Soc. Rev. 42: 905-920.

EDELHERTZ, H. (1970) The Nature, Impact and Prosecution of White-Collar Crime. Washington, DC: National Institute of Law Enforcement and Criminal Justice.

FABERMAN, H. A. (1975) "A criminogenic market structure: the automobile industry." Soc. Q. 16: 438-457.

GETSCHOW, G. (1979) "Some middle managers cut corners to achieve high corporate goals." Wall Street J. (November 8).

GREEN, M. (1978) The Other Government: The Unseen Power of Washington Lawyers. New York: Norton.

—— B. C. MOORE, Jr., and B. WASSERSTEIN (1972) The Closed Enterprise System. New York: Norton.

GREENBERG, D. F. (1977a) "Socioeconomic status and criminal sentences: is there an association?" Amer. Soc. Rev. 42: 174-176.

—— (1977b) "The dynamics of oscillatory punishment processes." J. of Criminal Law and Criminology 68: 643-651.

GROSS, E. (1978) "Organizations as criminal actors," pp. 199-213 in P. R. Wilson and J. Braithwaite (eds.) Two Faces of Deviance: Crimes of the Powerless and Powerful. Brisbane: Univ. of Queensland Press.

HAGAN, J. (1974) "Extra-legal attributes and criminal sentencing: an assessment of a sociological viewpoint." Law and Society Rev. 8: 357-383.

—— and I. H. NAGEL BURNSTEIN (1979) "The sentencing bargaining of upperworld and underworld crime in ten federal district courts." Law and Society Rev. 13: 467-478.

—— and C. ALBONETTI (1980) "The differential sentencing of white-collar offenders in ten federal district courts." Amer. Soc. Rev. 45: 802-820.

Harvard Law Review (1979) "Developments in the Law: Corporate crime: regulating corporate behavior through criminal sanctions." Harvard Law Rev. 92: 1229-1375.

HOPKINS, A. (1977) "Is there a class bias in criminal sanctioning?" Amer. Soc. Rev. 42: 176-177.

HUTT, P. (1973) "The philosophy of regulation under the federal Food, Drug and Cosmetic Act." Food, Drug and Cosmetic Law J. 28: 177.

JACOBY, N. H., P. NEHEMKIS, and R. EELLS (1977) Bribery and Extortion in World Business. New York: Macmillan.

JANKOVIC, I. (1977) "Punishment and the post-industrial society: a study of unemployment, crime and imprisonment in the United States." Ph.D. dissertation, University of California, Santa Barbara.

KENNEDY, T. and C. E. SIMON (1978) An Examination of Questionable Payments and Practices. New York: Praeger.

KNIGHTLEY, P., H. EVANS, E. POTTER, and M. WALLACE (1979) Suffer the Children: The Story of Thalidomide. New York: Viking.

KRIESBERG, S. M. (1976) "Decisionmaking models and the control of corporate crime." Yale Law J. 85: 1091-1129.

LEONARD, W. N. and M. G. WEBER (1970) "Automakers and dealers: a study of criminogenic market forces." Law and Society Rev. 4: 407-424.

LEVIN, M. H. (1977) "Crimes against employees: substantive criminal sanctions under the Occupational Safety and Health Act." Amer. Criminal Law Rev. 14: 717-745.

LEWIS-BECK, M. S. and J. R. ALFORD (1980) "Can government regulate safety? The coal mine example." Amer. Pol. Sci. Rev. 74: 745-756.

LISKA, A. E. and M. TAUSIG (1979) "Theoretical interpretations of social class and racial differentials in legal decision-making for juveniles." Soc. Q. 20: 197-207.

LIZOTTE, A. J. (1978) "Extra-legal factors in Chicago's criminal courts: testing the conflict model of criminal justice." Social Problems 25: 564-580.

MORRIS, N. (1974) The Future of Imprisonment. Chicago: Univ. of Chicago Press.

NEEDLEMAN, M. L. and C. NEEDLEMAN (1979) "Organizational crime: two models of criminogenesis." Soc. Q. 20: 517-528.

O'CONNOR, J. (1973) The Fiscal Crisis of the State. New York: St. Martin's.

OGREN, R. W. (1973) "The ineffectiveness of the criminal sanction in fraud and corruption cases: losing the battle against white-collar crime." Amer. Criminal Law Rev. 11: 959-988.

PACKER, H. L. (1968) The Limits of the Criminal Sanction. Stanford: Stanford Univ. Press.

POSNER, R. A. (1976) Antitrust Law: An Economic Perspective. Chicago: Univ. of Chicago Press.

QUINNEY, R. (1977) Class, State and Crime. New York: David McKay.

—— (1963) "Occupational structure and criminal behavior: prescription violation by retail pharmacists." Social Problems 11: 179-185.

RAAB, S. (1980) "Ex-owner says mob took over chemicals firm." New York Times (November 24).

REIMAN, J. H. (1979) The Rich Get Richer and the Poor Get Prison. New York: John Wiley.

REISMAN, W. M. (1979) Folded Lies: Bribery, Crusades and Reforms. New York: Free Press.

ROSSI, P. H., E. WAITE, C. E. BOSE, and R. E. BERK (1974) "The seriousness of crimes: normative structure and individual differences." Amer. Soc. Rev. 39: 224-237.

RUTTER, M. and N. MADGE (1976) Cycles of Disadvantage. London: Heinemann.

SAXON, M. S. (1980) White-Collar Crime: The Problem and the Federal Response. Washington, DC: Congressional Research Service, Library of Congress.

SCHRAG, P. G. (1971) "On Her Majesty's Secret Service: protecting the consumer in New York City." Yale Law J. 80: 1529-1603.

SCHRAGER, L. S. and J. F. SHORT, Jr. (1980) "How serious a crime? Perceptions of organizational and common crimes," pp. 14-31 in G. Geis and E. Stotland (eds.) White-Collar Crime: Theory and Research. Beverly Hills, CA: Sage.

SCOTT, J. E. and F. AL-THAKEB (1977) "The public's perceptions of crime: a comparative analysis of Scandinavia, Western Europe, the Middle East, and the United States," pp. 78-88 in C. R. Huff (ed.) Contemporary Corrections. Beverly Hills, CA: Sage.

SCOTT, R. (1974) Muscle and Blood. New York: E. P. Dutton.

STONE, C. (1975) Where the Law Ends: The Social Control of Corporate Behavior. New York: Harper & Row.

SUTHERLAND, E. H. (1949) White-Collar Crime. New York: Holt, Rinehart & Winston.

TAFT, D. R. (1966) "Influence on the general culture on crime." Federal Probation 30: 15-23.

WOLFGANG, M. E. (1980) National Survey of Crime Severity Final National Level Geometric Means and Ratio Scores by Offense Stimuli Items. University of Pennsylvania. (mimeo)

YEAGER, M. G. (1979) "Unemployment and imprisonment." J. of Criminal Law and Criminology 70: 586-588.

Arnold Anderson-Sherman
George Mason University

5

THE SOCIAL CONSTRUCTION
OF "TERRORISM"

The U.S. government has recently attempted to make the elimination of "international terrorism" a major policy thrust (GIST, December 1980). One technique adopted to achieve this goal is to fashion national and international agreements that "terrorism" is a crime (Current Policy, No. 340, October 29, 1981). The assumption is that by creating such laws and agreements, along with necessary enforcement mechanisms, this problem can be brought under control. This is an instance of governments limiting social control to defining a problem as a crime and attempting to eradicate the problem by arresting and punishing perpetrators.

This chapter examines a historical case of "terrorist" activity: the so-called Mau Mau movement. It moves between levels of analysis from the highly abstract to the fairly specific. Various models will be outlined briefly. Then the case will be presented, with some links back to theory. The tribal life of the Kikuyu in the later part of the nineteenth century prior to the coming of British dominance will be described, followed by the British takeover from the 1880s through the 1940s, and the rise of Mau Mau in the 1950s. Finally, the argument and its implications will be presented.

AUTHOR'S NOTE: For helpful comments I wish to thank K. Avruch, H. Berringer, P. Black, T. Hickey, H. Pepinsky, M. Schlueter, J. Scimecca, and T. Williams.

The case of Mau Mau provides an opportunity to use a combination of theoretical perspectives to understand the dialectical relation between social movements and polities in the context of the world political economy. It also provides an opportunity to demonstrate that the new combined perspective allows for powerful social diagnosis, which has the potential for policy analysis and application. Certainly it is capable of demystifying public policy based on ideological understandings.

Events might have gone differently had both sides recognized it was in the interest of the British to define Mau Mau activity in the 1950s as other than "terrorist." The historical record shows such a possibility existed. The United States is in a similar situation today. Attempts to label acts of violence by nonpolity groups as terrorism exists because of, and creates, social blindness. Some acts of terrorism may best be treated as criminal acts, but others may not. The use of criminal law creation and implementation as a solution to problems derives from an ideological stance in which generalized assumptions about pluralistic democratic practices operate without adequate diagnosis of how the world actually operates (Current Policy, October 29, 1981).

It is ironic that the need for adequate diagnosis has actually been called for by Rostow (Washington Post, January, 1982). Rostow argues that a key problem of American foreign policy is the absence of informed diagnosis by intellectuals. This statement is ironic because it is made at a time when it is increasingly difficult for academicians to obtain either the government financing or information that would provide a partial basis for such a diagnosis. The result is policy that may seem pragmatic but that is probably self-defeating expediency.

Rostow's statement is also ironic because contemporary policy makers often claim that even if sociological analysis could help in achieving understanding, such knowledge cannot be transformed into effective policy. The claim is that sociological knowledge does not tell us what to do in the here and now. It is important to consider that claim.

THEORETICAL PERSPECTIVES

Defining "Terrorism"—The World Taken for Granted

The problem of understanding modern terrorism stems from a number of factors (Anderson-Sherman, 1982). These include failure to achieve a universally accepted definition of "terrorism." This is clearly seen at multidisciplinary meetings where experts provide a variety of definitions and, after failure to achieve common agreement, go on to discuss different phenomena. This is not the case of the blind men and the elephant, as it is not clear that the international experts even have hold of the same beast. The variety of entities included under the rubric "terrorist" includes acts of "criminals," psychotics, and acts of violence by those acting within a social movement directed toward national independence, as well as state "terrorism," or "terrorism from above."

To define "terrorism" or "terrorist acts" as crimes creates a process of reification which may produce undesired and unanticipated consequences. The a priori definition of "terrorism" as evil assumes, among other things, that terrorism is a zero-sum game. "Terrorism"-"counter-terrorism" may in fact exist in situations that can be converted from zero-sum to mixed-sum games (Burton, 1979). The case of Mau Mau may have been such an instance.

Politicians understand the notion of worlds-taken-for-granted. Such worlds are constructed from the cultural residue of the worlds of our ancestors, as we shall see in the case of the Kikuyu and the British. People daily construct, deconstruct, and reconstruct the world (Berger and Luckmann, 1967). The point is not that one man's terrorist is another's freedom fighter, but that yesterday's terrorist is today's statesman, and today's statesman may become tomorrow's terrorist. Jomo Kenyatta is only one of many examples. It is important to understand this process.

The product of terror is designed at times to disrupt, and at times to maintain, worlds taken for granted. The art of politics includes the ability to define an action in ways that make sense in terms of achieving a desired outcome (Rosenblum, 1982). When political "terror" is defined as an act of political violence, it may make sense because that definition may help to achieve certain ends. The rational response may be to call the opponents' violent political act irrational and to label them inhuman. Thus it becomes possible to command "rational" support for aggressive counteraction. Since "they only understand force and have to be contained," often for their own good, it is they, not we, who are the cause of our own violent response. In foreign affairs this is called policy. For an individual it is a defense mechanism called projection.

Understanding the importance of proper criteria of definition (Gittler, 1977) makes possible the kind of objective analysis Rostow has called for. In attempting to free ourselves from our own ideological perspectives, the attempt can begin to unravel the subtle network of factors at work. Social diagnosis begins when the risk of confusing symbols with reality is minimized. The following additional perspectives seem useful and will be stated briefly.

Wallerstein's political world-economy model (PEWS) informs the analysis of Britain as a core power reacting to changes created by the opening of the Suez Canal. The relation of the British and the Kikuyu is part of a process that started with the voyages of exploration. The PEWS approach focuses on the world-system rather than nation-states. Competition between core powers for hegemony in capital accumulation based on extraction of raw resources and/or cheap labor from geopolitically secure areas turns out to be an important aspect of developments in Kenya.

Theories of social movements (Tilly, 1978; Paige, 1975; McAdam, 1982; Zald and McCarthy, 1980) examine interaction between challenging movements and polities. But in the case of Mau Mau the polity is at the core while the challenger is in the periphery. Despite this difference, the political process and resource mobilization models sensitize us to look at interests, organization, resources, opportunity, tolerance, repression, and power. States, for example, may be more or less repressive and may allow opportunity for collective action or decrease opportunity through threat. At the same time, however, an increase in threat may escalate movement activity. An example is provided by the British Declaration of 1952 and the subsequent movement of the Kikuyu into the mountains.

Bendix (1978) says that modern revolutions tend to justify authority by popular mandate. Authority and inequality are based both on "power and the mandate to rule" (Bendix, 1978: 6). The claim to legitimacy and use of force were important parts of the conflict in Kenya. The ability to define a violent political action as produced by Freedom Fighters or terrorists is fundamentally a question of legitimacy. Societies adapt to such universal conditions as popular mandate according to their unique history. But Bendix's notion of the role of ideas (mandate, legitimacy) in explaining order and change is critical. Ideas are carried by intellectuals, like Kenyatta. The idea of elites and masses and the ways they are formed and change, or resist change, is important in terms of the social construction of reality. It is the notion of unique differences between societies and the possibility of ideas having an effect that provide a fulcrum for social policy analysis in this case.

This chapter is also informed by theories of techniques of dominance and minority reactions to dominance that have been developed in the field of ethnicity. The combination of PEWS and social movements models may help in understanding the conditions under which various alternatives are used.

The aggressive terrorist reaction of the Mau Mau movement falls within what Paige (1975) called peasant revolutions. Paige is concerned with how large areas of the Third World were affected by the development of a world market for agricultural commodities (1975: x). Paige notes that in "Peru, Angola, Vietnam and many other areas of the underdeveloped world the United States has chosen to side with the landlords and plantation owners against the peasants, sharecroppers, and agricultural workers who took up arms against them" (p. x).

At a time when U.S. foreign policy is to condemn all terrorist activity out of hand, it is useful to be informed by these theoretical perspectives as we look at how the British dealt with terrorism when they were the dominant core society. Future analysis will have to examine convergence and divergence in these theoretical models in greater detail, as well as to examine a variety of social movements in which peripheral societies react against the core. In the meantime, this chapter serves as an illustration of the complex causes of at least one time of terrorist activity and shows the possibility of an overly ideological and rigid response on the part of core powers.

The Kikuyu

Kikuyu culture and social structure are integrated. Key elements are family, clan, and the age-grading of members of the same birth cohort. This is an important difference from individual age-dating from birth, as is done in the West. Individualism among the Kikuyu is secondary to membership in the tribe. Role obligations are clear. There are sanctions for conformity and deviance. Change in social status is accompanied by rituals in which oaths are taken. The taking of oaths is tied to taboo social practices to make them more significant and binding.

The basic social unit is the family. The family widens by a "natural process of growth and division" (Kenyatta, 1962: 297). The symbol of the kinship bond is the family land. Land is not only a symbol but the key to the autonomous horticultural subsistence economy of this basically vegetarian people. The whole social organization derives from the relation of social units to the land.

Preparation for complex social life takes place through education. Kikuyu children learn by experience and are given work within their ability. They begin to contribute at an early age. This is but one basic difference from European culture. Technical aspects of socialization are acquired within the age group. Other aspects of culture are learned within the family, unlike European education, which separates the individual from the family and creates a relationship of the individual to the state. This provides the basis for later movement organization. Yet there are also cultural similarities. Children, for example, learn equality, cooperation, and democratic competition. These similarities are pointed out by Kenyatta.

As age groups rise within the social hierarchy, their progress is marked by a series of initiation rites and ceremonies based on common understandings. One of the most important is the circumcision ceremony, which moves members of the age-grade to a marriageable status. Since the family is the basis of social organization, marriage and courtship are of special importance. Marriage takes place on the basis of free choice within the tribe, but it is also important in terms of creating family linkages—again, the basis for movement organization as well as a possible link for intercultural cooperation.

Marriage is a further step toward adulthood. Kenyatta notes (1963: 303) that it "is not until he has a family" that a man has "a chance to show his capacity for wise administration and for dealing intelligently and justly with people." If he has demonstrated this, then by the time he has children entering adolescence he may be chosen from his age group as one "mature enough to take part in . . . tribal government." Such an individual is expected to act on the "interests of the community" as he has for his family. An individual showing these qualities is likely to be selected "by the elders as one who will play an important part in public affairs later on, but not until he has passed successive age-grades" and acquired the experience that will qualify him to take full responsibility in tribal matters. By that time he is probably the leader of almost a miniature tribe of his own relatives, as well as his age-grade, and his family life will give evidence of his ability in government" (Kenyatta, 1962: 303). This shows the integrated nature of Kikuyu society, the elements of their culture which might have made accommodation with the British possible, and the basis on which the revolutionary leadership would emerge.

But this is from the analytic perspective. Seen through British eyes, various aspects of Kikuyu life seen separately did not make sense. Oath taking, circumcision practices, and polygamy confirmed to the British that the Kikuyu were savages. Let's look again at these practices from an analytic perspective.

Since the basis of social unity is the family, large families are important. Men have the number of wives they can support. The more wives, the more children. Both male and female children are useful in production. Females are the connecting link between generations. Males are important in terms of war. The taking of a second wife is often initiated by the first wife who sees subsequent wives not as threats but as companions and co-workers. Husbands, as well as each wife, have their own hut. The times when the male visits each of his wives is strictly controlled by custom; thus jealousy is minimized. Since typically there were more females than males between the ages of 15 and 20, when most Kikuyu marry, polygamy had the interesting side effect that all women married. As a result there is no word in the language for spinster or prostitute.

Kikuyu social organization provides the organizational base for the Mau Mau movement. The oaths and initiation rites become the basis for movement solidarity. The misperception of the social nature of oaths and the practice of circumcision by the British contributed to reactions that were part of the causal process that led to Mau Mau and blinded the British to alternative scenarios.

THE COMING OF THE BRITISH

There is a difference between a symbol and an act. Taking property does not always become theft; taking life does not always become murder. Whether an act becomes a crime is partly conditioned by who controls the media and the government.

Prior to 1850 there was little contact between Europeans and Kikuyu. In terms of the political world-economy model the Kikuyu were in an area external to the system and had not yet been peripheralized. By the 1850s sporadic contact began to occur. But it was not until the opening of the Suez Canal in 1869 that the race for East Africa accelerated. Controlling the headwaters of the Nile, located in Uganda, came to have great geopolitical significance. To control Uganda a viable railroad line was necessary to a seaport. The path from Uganda to the nearest possible seaport, Mombasa, led straight through Kikuyuland.

The British brought to East Africa a policy of making the colonies pay their own way. In some cases minerals or an export crop was the basis for such payment. But the Kikuyu had no minerals or crops of commercial interest. The interest of the British in Kikuyuland was for the rail route needed to protect control of the Nile. For this the tribes in that area had to be subdued, and the administrative apparatus necessary for operating the rail line had to be in place. Since the Kikuyu could not pay the costs of building the railroad or for the British Colonial Administration it was decided to open the land for settlement by whites. This involves the assumption that this is unoccupied land which is "up for grabs."

Into the land of the Kikuyu came the English settlers. Like colonists everywhere they brought with them beliefs that defined the land as uninhabited, the people as barbarians, and their religion as heathen. Based on these beliefs, developed since the earliest voyages of discovery and continuing to this day, they took over the land they defined not only as free but as underutilized. By doing so they transformed a landed agricultural group into alienated wage-laborers and serfs.

This was done by a series of policies and laws. The government and the settlers worked purposively to drive natives off their land and to create a class of urban wage laborers. To do this they used taxation, low wages, land appropriation, restriction on cash crops, laws, and force. The restriction of cash crops made it necessary for a larger number of family members to leave the land and take wage-laborer jobs to pay hut and poll taxes. This freed the land for settlement. Later many of these acts would be the basis for grievances by Kikuyu associations.

In order for the British to carry out this policy in a way that did not damage their self-esteem, they saw themselves as acting for the well-being of the African. The Africans had their own perception of reality, as indicated in this story told by a young Kikuyu man about a conversation he had as a boy with his grandfather:

'Do you see those big blue gum trees on a line at the edge of the forest?' he asked me, pointing to some Eucalyptus trees. 'Yes grandfather.' 'Those trees were planted by your great uncle, my elder son, on his third year after his circumcision. They mark the boundary between the Native Reserve and the Forest Reserve which is under Government control. All the land west of those trees was alienated by Government in 1910. By that time we had a lot of millet growing where you see those blue gum trees growing inside the forest. Today we are forbidden to collect firewood from that forest which was ours; we are not allowed to cut even strings for binding together wood when building a hut. Do you see that small hut under the tree?' 'Yes, grandfather.' 'That is the Forest Guard's hut. It is built on my step-brother's land, Gateru. The boundary went through his land leaving him with only a small portion. Today if the Forest Guards catch a person with any forest property, he would be accused and fined or imprisoned.

We buy or work for firewood and all building materials from our former lands which the European has not planted or taken care of.

'My grandson, there is nothing as bad on this earth as a lack of power' [Barnett, 1966: 86].

The grandson would grow up to become a general in the movement. The British saw themselves as bringing civilization to the native. Having heard the voice of a Kikuyu grandfather, listen to the voice of a colonial administrator:

> The reaction of a native race to control by a civilized government varies according to the nature, and to the form of government, but in every case a conflict of some kind is inevitable, before the lower race fully accepts the dictum of the ruling power. It may come quickly or it may be postponed, and it is often better if it comes quickly [Mungeam, 1966: 277].

The view of the British military in East Africa was congruent with the view of this administrator. The goal is to win as quickly as possible with the fewest casualties. As one soldier states: "In my view, any means to achieve those ends are justified. In the long run, inflicting heavy casualties on an enemy will shorten the duration of the conflict, it will teach a lesson and will result in a more enduring peace than less violent means" (Mungeam, 1966: 277).

The Kikuyu Response (Pluralism: 1900-1945)

Political process theory (Tilly, 1978; McAdam, 1982) says to look for social organization in judging the resources of a social movement. Kikuyu tribal organization provided one basis for the Mau Mau social movement. The British provided an additional basis with the common experience of many East African tribes, including that of transformation into wage-laborers. The result was a rise of political consciousness among the Kikuyu and the development of a variety of Kikuyu organizations, such as the Kikuyu Association, the Young Kikuyu Association, and the East African Association. These organizations began to emerge in the early 1920s.

For the most part these organizations adopted British democratic-pluralist ideology. They brought grievances to various commissions and sought redress through democratic means. In each case the findings went against them.

Strong dissent also started early. In 1922 Thuku attacked the government for "stealing Kikuyu land" (Barnett, 1966: 36). As Tilly noted, the extent to which the polity is tolerant or repressive in reaction to protest plays an important role in the development of social movements. Thus the decision to arrest Thuku and hold him for "deportation on charges of being 'dangerous to peace and good order'" (Barnett, 1966: 37) was an important decision, a decision which adequate analysis might have avoided.

The arrest of Thuku was followed by a general strike. The subsequent series of events is reminiscent of Kent State:

> Several thousand Africans, largely Kikuyu, gathered in protest outside Nairobi jail where Thuku was being held and demanded the release of their leader. The police, frightened and tense, perhaps by this unexpected show of African strength, responded to a shot fired by one of their members by opening fire on the crowd. When the shooting had stopped, Twenty-one Africans lay dead on the street and a much larger number were injured [Barnett, 1966: 37].

Still there was a press toward the use of pluralistic processes. Demands of indigenous organizations included (1) title to deeds of African held land, as well as

> (2) the return of alienated land, or just compensation, (3) removal of restrictions on the planting by Africans of commercial crops, . . . (4) the training and employment of Africans as agricultural instructors, (5) compulsory primary education for African children, sufficient secondary and high schools, and opportunities for higher education . . . , (6) abolition of the *kipande* system, exemption of women from Hut and Poll Taxes, and removal of other measures which restricted freedom of movement or compelled Africans to leave their *shambas* (gardens) to work for Europeans, and (7) elected representation in the Legislative Council, as well as in other governing bodies, and a promise of ultimate African predominance [Barnett, 1966: 37-38].

Many of these demands could have been met without feeling that the land had been turned over to the rebels.

Instead, organizations like the Kikuyu Central Association were declared illegal. The KCA was declared illegal in 1940. The Kenya African Union was formed in 1944 and in 1946 its aims were for democratic reform. We find a small number of intellectuals as members of many associations and a cross-linkage between organizations. In time this would contribute to the formation of a single movement. By the 1950s hopes for democratic reform were gone. It was becoming clear that constitutional means were ineffective.

The Mau Mau Revolt: 1952-1956

Part of the recruitment mechanism had its roots in Kikuyu culture and included a terrible oath. This oath was made illegal. On May 31, 1950 "nineteen Africans . . . were accused . . . of having administered an illegal oath binding its takers to a secret Mau Mau association. In August of the same year, this society was officially proscribed" (Barnett, 1966: 51). Note that the term "Mau Mau" has no literal meaning in Kikuyu or in Swahili. In view of disembodied cultural traits such as the oath, the Kikuyu as a people were ignored and the manufactured entity of Mau Mau was given the connotation of barbarism and savagery in the Western mind. The press focused on isolated acts of violence. The following article from the *New York Times* of September 29, 1952 presents a typical treatment of a Mau Mau raid:

NEW RAIDS IN KENYA

Dread Mau Mau Native Group Kills 2 African Chiefs
Nairobi, Kenya, Sept. 28 (AP)—The police announced today the murderous native Mau Mau society had struck again, killing two African chieftains and slaughtering 350 cattle and sheep owned by white settlers in the foothills of Mount Kenya.

The latest blow of the anti-white society—sworn to drive the British out of Africa—took place while the colonial legislature was considering emergency laws to crack down on the terrorists.

The raided district is about 1000 miles from Nairobi. The Mau Mau struck after a night meeting, slaughtering the livestock with spears, swords, and knives. They cut telegraph lines to hamper police action, but authorities said about 100 suspected members had already been rounded up [quoted in Paige, 1975: 96-97].

Meanwhile, increasing numbers of people were in jail or awaiting trial for being suspected members of the Mau Mau organization.

Starting in the early 1950s there were random acts of violence, probably initiated by local leaders. Such acts may have been partly related to the initiation oaths by movement members. Many historians mark the declaration of a state of emergency on October 20, 1952 and the subsequent movement into the forests to avoid arrest as the transformation point of dissent from a pluralist challenge to an effective social movement (Barnett, 1966: 69).

Instead of pursuing the Africans into the forest and following the process which ultimately led to independence in Kenya in 1962, we turn to some of the implications of the events considered so far.

THE ROAD NOT TAKEN

This chapter examined Kikuyu tribal life and the mind sets of the British Colonial Administrators, members of the Imperial British East Africa Company, and the settlers. The political-economic context in which the British operated was set forth. These factors, in the context of political world economy and political process models, help explain the development of the so-called Mau Mau movement. We saw how the actions of members of some African tribes, particularly the Kikuyu tribe, were transformed by the Western press into the Mau Mau terrorists and how the conflict led to Kenyan independence and contributed to the end of the British Empire.

The British tried to label activities of members of the Kikuyu tribe as criminal; yet these activities were in large part caused by the actions of the British themselves. Other scenarios were possible.

For the British a key interest was the railroad. Increased coffee production to help defray costs was a secondary interest. The cost of immediate implementation of the secondary interest contributed to the destruction of Kikuyu tribal life. Yet from the early period of 1920 and onward it was clear that the Kikuyu were more capable of assimilating aspects of British culture than the British understood. From the formation of the KCA in 1920 the educated Kikuyu were operating partly within democratic and pluralist traditions.

At an early point many Kikuyu recognized the advantages association with the British would offer. It seems possible that either not importing settlers or not supporting them once they had been imported could have met British goals. The railway could have been built and protected. Eventual improvement in the economic infrastructure might even have helped pay for this venture. The Africans might have maintained land tenure and their tribal life yet adopted modern techniques. In fact, this was one of their demands. A small cost would have been some modernization. The cost to the British would have been slower capital accumulation, but they might have retained their geopolitical interest. The Kikuyu would have gained economically.

Thus, bringing in settlers and creating the hut and poll taxes were policy errors. Still at subsequent points there was room for alternatives. The key error was the government decree that was supposed to finally quash the movement. Instead this was the precipitating stroke that galvanized dissent and mobilized organization. The attempt to legislate solutions to problems which are not understood may produce unanticipated and undesirable results.

One implication of analysis of the case of Kenya is that the present policy of the United States to attempt to treat all terrorism as a crime and allow access to data only to those who share this understanding limits exploration of alternative solutions and makes the world a less rational and more dangerous place to live.

Much of politics is conflict over scarce resources and the infrastructure necessary to accumulate and protect those resources. This was clear in the British takeover of East Africa. Those who argue that politics can be examined only at the level of the nation-state have a limited perspective, as the political world-economy model makes clear. The danger, if not the inhumanity, of this limitation is clearly seen in contemporary cases. More levels of complexity besides the nation-state are involved. We see this with the resurgence of ethnic identity, religious insurgency, and independence movements throughout the contemporary world (Clark, 1980).

Science does not produce generalizations that help predict the future for this kind of data, although this is arguable. But the data do sensitize us to variables that need to be addressed by social diagnosticians regardless of their social location (university or government agency).

In the long run the conflict in East Africa was resolved not by democratic processes but by violent conflict. From a rigid political world-economy perspective this may be seen as an overriding historical process which is repeated again and again; the choices ranging from annihilation of the tribe to revolution from below. But there is a certain charm to the notion (Bendix, 1978; Scimecca, 1981) that ideas and volition allow human choice within the historical and social context. This understanding of the Kikuyu social revolution shows the importance of taking a dispassionate view of a particular social situation before making a judgment. A violent political act often cannot best be viewed in isolation from the worldwide social and historical context which led to that particular violent moment in time.

Bendix appears to be right about the importance of popular mandate in modern times. Some Africans and intellectuals did play the role Bendix described. But in many cases the idea of mandate by, or for, the people is a defense mechanism, a rationalization for one's beliefs. Acting in the name of the people may be a technique for control of the masses. We know that media often support the government in manipulating public opinion.

Here is a case where government and press worked together to label a movement as terrorism. If Mau Mau existed today, it might be one of the phenomena to be covered under laws to criminalize terrorism. It is necessary to find new solutions to these problems. A start is to pick up the point made by Rostow. Agencies involved in considering terrorism might make data accessible for impartial investigation. Certainly social and historical analyses provide a basis for understanding. Means other than force are available; these include mediation, negotiation, and arbitration. What is clearly counterproductive is the blindness created by premature labeling and classification.

SUMMARY AND CONCLUSIONS

Such analysis must distinguish efforts to create laws which try to treat all of these groups in the same way. The cost to society of social movements that use terrorist activity is possible political instability. The cost of criminal activity involves loss of life and property but may not be dangerous to polity. The cost of repression to contain such events may be high not only economically but in terms of democracy and freedom (Bell, 1978). And while locking up criminals could conceivably have some effect, the repression might be of use for challengers in a political sense. Certainly this was true in Kenya in October 1952.

The United States has come a long way in terms of attempts to reify all terrorism as crime. How can it back off? This requires distinguishing types of terrorist acts and working not to avoid terrorist activity so much as to dispel the terror produced.

The task of solving problems by deconstructing worlds taken for granted includes not assuming a priori that a situation is either zero-sum or mixed-sum. The process of conflict management includes reconceptualizing what appeared to be zero-sum games into mixed-sum results. Often, in fact, the intent of the terrorist is to convince those who think they are in a powerful zero-sum position that in fact they are in error. Many situations may not be zero-sum except by social construction and may be transformed into situations where each side is able to see the world as taken for granted by others as well as themselves. Such knowledge, based on a broader world view, can lead to mediated settlements where in a new world taken for granted each side wins (Burton, 1980). We do not know, and cannot know, if that was possible in Kenya. Yet the structural analysis engaged in above certainly indicates a number of alternative scenarios to the one that became history.

The assumption of political ideologies such as pluralism as a stance also contributes to social constructions that stand in the way of solutions. Thinking about terrorism as rational political action is proscribed by those who assume pluralist conditions exist. It should not simply be asumed that participants have the ability to protect their interest through the use of peaceful institutional mechanisms. The assumption of pluralists of their own objectivity is also a contributing reification that fails to provide a framework for adequate diagnosis. The assumption of the availability of democratic means leaves pluralists in the position of condemning nongovernmental use of force on an a priori basis.

If solutions are to be found through law, then the generic behavior needs to be addressed; in this case the subject is the production of terror through violent means regardless of whether it is from above or below. The case of the British and the Kikuyu saw a minority group adopt the ideology of pluralism and attempt for many years to use democratic means to achieve redress of their grievances. The stated policy of British administrators and soldiers included the use of force to maintain order. If universal principles are to be applied, they must be applied universally in order to achieve a popular mandate. But in the long run the case of the Kikuyu shows that what is needed is less reification of particularistic self-interest and more adequate diagnosis of the alternative possibilities contained within particular sociohistorical contexts.

Understanding social phenomena using these tools provides part of what is necessary for social understanding, demystification, and alternative policies. Analysts should not lose sight of the variety of potential futures available at any moment in time. Complex diagnosis helps. The sociology of knowledge perspective is useful, as is the realization that ideas play a role not only in understanding but in action. Kenyatta understood this better than the British.

It seems that the closer people get to the sources of power, the more real their words seem to themselves and others. This is in part because they think they have a monopoly on converting words into reality. They have evidence that people act on their words and things either happen or are blocked. From their perspective the words of academics are less powerful—empty, in fact—because there is no force behind them (Greisman, 1977).

Yet in 1938 Jomo Kenyatta published a book that can be read on three levels: as a respectable piece of anthropology meant to impress peers and mentors, as a message to the British providing information about how a negotiated and mutually satisfactory agreement could be reached, and as a handbook for revolutionary organization.

In 1952 The British imposed the declaration prohibiting the administration of the Mau Mau oath. Many Kikuyu started moving into the mountains, from which they would launch a revolutionary movement that would win UHURU (freedom) for Kenya and would help drive the British from Africa and out of the core. The title of Kenyatta's book was *Facing Mount Kenya.*

REFERENCES

AARONOVITCH, S. (1947) Crisis in Kenya. London: Lawrence and Wishart.

ANDERSON-SHERMAN, A. (1981) "Toward a definition of terrorism." Presented at the London School of Economics and Political Science, November 16.

BARNETT, D. L. and K. NJAMI (1966) Mau Mau from Within: Autobiography and Analysis of Kenya's Peasant Revolt. New York: Monthly Review Press.

BELL, J. (1978) A Time of Terror: How Democratic Societies Respond to Revolutionary Violence. New York: Basic Books.

BENDIX, R. (1978) Kings or People: Power and the Mandate to Rule. Berkeley: Univ. of California Press.

BERGER, P. L. and T. LUCKMANN (1967) The Social Construction of Reality. Garden City, NY: Doubleday.

BURTON, J. (1979) Deviance, Terrorism & War. New York: St. Martin's.

CLARK. R. P. (1980) "Euzkadi: Basque nationalism in Spain since the Civil War," in C. R. Foster (ed.) Nations Without a State: Ethnic Minorities in Western Europe. New York.

CORFIELD, F. D. (1960) Historical Survey of Origins and Growth of Mau-Mau. London: H.M.S.O.

GIST (1980) Washington, DC: Bureau of Public Affairs, Department of State (December).

GITTLER, J. (1977) "Toward defining an ethnic minority." Int. J. of Group Tensions.

GREISMAN, H. C. (1977) "Social meanings of terrorism: reification, violence, and social control." Contemporary Crises 1: 303-318.

GUTKIND, P.C.W. and I. WALLERSTEIN [eds.] (1976) The Political Economy of Contemporary Africa. Beverly Hills, CA: Sage.

HUXLEY. E. and M. PERHAM (1975) Race and Politics in Kenya. Westport, CT: Greenwood.

KENYATTA, J. (1962) Facing Mount Kenya. New York: Vintage Books.

LEAKEY, L.S.B. (1953) Mau Mau and the Kikuyu. London: Methuen.

McADAM, D. (1970) Political Process in the Development of Black Insurgency, 1930-1970. Chicago: Univ. of Chicago Press.

MITCHELL, R. C. and H. TURNER (1966) Bibliography of Modern African Religious Movements. New York: Evanston.

MUNGEAM, G. H. (1966) British Rule in Kenya 1895-1912: The Establishment of Administration in the East Africa Protectorate. Oxford: Clarendon Press.

MURRAY-BROWN, J. (1973) Kenyatta. New York: E.P. Dutton.

PAIGE, J. M. (1975) Agrarian Revolution: Social Movements and Export Agriculture in the Underdeveloped World. New York: Free Press.

ROSBERG, C. and J. NOTHINGHAM (1966) The Myth of Mau-Mau Nationalism in Kenya. New York: Praeger.

ROSENBLUM, K. E. (1982) "The power of Richard Nixon, now you see it, now you don't. Three presidential press conferences as a study in the informal negotiation of deviance. Eastern Sociological Society Meetings, March.

ROSTOW. W. W. (1982) Article in The Washington Post, January 23, p. A3.

SCIMECCA, J. A. (1981) Society and Freedom. New York: St. Martin's.

STONEHARM, I. T. (1953) Mau-Mau. London: British Museum Press.

TILLY, C. (1978) From Mobilization to Revolution. Reading, MA: Addison-Wesley.

WALLERSTEIN, I. (1974) The Modern World-System: Capitalist Agriculture and the Origins of the European World-Economy in the Sixteenth Century. New York: Academic Press.

ZALD, M. N. and J. D. McCARTHY [eds.] (1979) The Dynamics of Social Movements. Cambridge: Withrop.

Joseph Harrison
Nashville, Tennessee

6

NEW EVIDENCE IN PSYCHOPHARMACOLOGY AS IT RELATES TO CRITICAL CRIMINOLOGY

DEFINING THE ISSUE

In any attempt to define the scope, goals, and purposes of critical criminology or of humanist sociology, one comes to recognize that the definitional task is somewhat analogous to attempting to divide a number by zero; you end up with a result that is a mixture between something infinite and something undefined. Despite the lack of agreement among sociologists—much less among criminologists—as to the proper nature and boundaries of their respective scholarly fields, critical criminologists and humanist sociologists seem to believe that there must be a sense of social and political consciousness associated with either a theory or an advocacy in criminology if either is to be ethically and theoretically acceptable. Toward this end we have exercised apprehensive restraint and concern when dealing with theories or empirical generalizations in our field which either limit or appear to limit the nature and freedom of the human endeavor in society. We do not approve of those theories which may accelerate coercive tactics or methods in society, whether those of legal, governmental, scientific, or academic origins. In this framework it is not surprising that most critical criminologists and praxis-oriented sociologists have been negative in their attitudes and evaluations toward sociobiological and psycho-

AUTHOR'S NOTE: An earlier version of this chapter was presented at the 1981 Annual Meetings of the Association for Humanist Sociology, Cincinnati.

biological elaborations of the causal processes leading to deviant behaviors. As one of those critical criminologists who believe that we should focus on the economic and political (rather than biological) etiologies of crime, I have spent considerable effort avoiding the dangers of simplistic sociobiological explanations of criminal behaviors.

Nevertheless, it is a necessary, albeit peculiar, role for critical criminologists at this moment to acknowledge and recognize that certain data within at least one field of sociobiology—the subcategory of psychopharmacology—is well worth looking at and cannot, indeed, be ignored any longer. If any consolation is required, one should be aware that inferences drawn from recent gathering and study of germane psychopharmacological data do not reveal any attack on our critical and humanistic inclinations toward sociology in general or toward criminology in particular.

The matters to be covered in this chapter include an outline of some of the interesting scientific findings of the last six years or so with regard to *endorphins,* and an integrated explanation of their significance on an empirical and on a theoretical level, with reference to a reasonable, even necessary, methodology for critical criminologists to follow in dealing with these kinds of scientific data. If scholars ignore this psychopharmacological evidence, they will allow control theorists and government bureaucrats (whom we can least trust to place the data in their proper perspectives) to take over the responsibility and power of determining its interpretation and use. If we leave it to others, the dangers of reductionism will materialize—that is, all human behaviors, deviant or otherwise, may eventually be reduced theoretically to biochemical correlates and neurotransmitters in action. This is *not* the underlying basis for all human behaviors in society, and it does not detract from political and economic analysis to also refer to pharmacological data. But it must be handled with care, and it must be addressed by critical theorists in criminology, not neglected as it has been thus far or relinquished to others' interpretations. Turning now to the topic of endorphins, these fascinating neuropeptides possess wide ranges of function in the human organism. While endorphins are not the only topic within sociobiology that could be addressed at this time, it is an area in which the relevance to criminology and to law is striking (Harrison, 1981).

THE PHARMACOLOGICAL EVIDENCE

Nearly a decade of frenzied research has resulted in the identification and classification of brain peptides whose effects in human beings resemble those of opiates such as morphine. The word "endorphin" is a contraction of *endo*genous mo*rphine*. Endorphins are constituent body chemicals found to exist naturally in all human beings and in many other animals, in the brain, pituitary gland, and gut (Ambinder and Schuster, 1979; Bloom and Segal, 1981). Endorphins attach themselves to the opiate receptors, specifically sculpted tissue sites to which exogenous narcotics (such as heroin or morphine) also attach themselves when humans receive such narcotics. Endorphins (a generic term that includes specific opiate peptides, including met-enkephalin, leuenkephalin, and beta-endorphin) appear virtually to duplicate completely the effects (physical and pharmacological) in human beings of narcotics which we have studied for many years, such as morphine, heroin, and other opium derivatives (Guillemin, 1978). When endorphins were discovered, the hope that they would produce the desired effects of morphine, such as analgesia, without the development of tolerance and dependence was quickly dashed by the recognition that endorphins can substitute for morphine in the suppression of withdrawal symptoms in morphine-dependent animals and humans and that, for all practical purposes, endorphins are our internal narcotics, possessing all of the key pharmacological characteristics of the external narcotics that the criminal law now regulates and that society in general tends to fear greatly (Bunney et al., 1979; Gold and Kleber, 1979; Snyder, 1979).

One of the most profound effects of opiates, both external ones such as heroin and natural internal ones such as beta-endorphin, is their analgesic effect (Olson et al., 1980). Regulation of pain perception is one likely role, therefore, for endorphins; another is the regulation of narcotic tolerance and dependence, as well as the control of various emotions (Blackwell, 1979; Catlin and Gorelick, 1980; Gold and Byck, 1979). The opiate tolerance, dependence, and withdrawal phenomena are regulated through the *locus coeruleus* of the brain and the activity of the *locus coeruleus* is inhibited by the presence of endorphins, thereby preventing withdrawal symptoms, even in humans who have been addicted to external narcotics and then stopped using those narcotics. Tolerance to and physical dependence on beta-endorphin has been clearly demonstrated (Ambinder and Schuster, 1979; Broccardo 1981; Bunney et al., 1979; Gold and Kleber, 1979; Guillemin, 1978). Endorphins share overlapping, if not completely identical, effects with morphine. These endorphin substances—which every human being possesses at every moment of his or her life—fit, by their characteristics, right into the guidelines of the Food and Drug Administration (FDA) and the Drug Enforcement Administration (DEA) for the classification and control of highly restricted substances under the 1970 Controlled Substances Act. Since all endorphins are opiates, with demonstrated tolerance and dependence, endorphins should—in theory—be viewed as Schedule I or Schedule II drugs within the Controlled Substances Act. The act sets up a five-schedule classification scheme, and opiates with no medical usages (e.g., heroin) fall into Schedule I, opiates with limited medical uses fall under Schedule II (e.g., morphine). Clearly, though, this classification of endorphins would be absurd. The Controlled Substances Act provides for criminal penalties for the unauthorized possession or sale of the narcotics it regulates; the paradox is evident when we understand that endorphins, despite their pharmacological narcotic properties, are a natural and physiological reality for all humans. Surely we could not be prosecuted for natural possession of these narcotic substances in our brains. Or could we?

We are addicted, every one of us, to our endorphins—our endogenous morphine. We are *all* "narcotic addicts." None of us could experience the loss of narcotics in our brains and bodies without experiencing severe withdrawal symptoms as a result. This conclusion appears to be justified and valid based on a wide variety of scientific experimentation (Bloom, 1981; Bunney et al., 1979; Carr and Bullen, 1981; Catlin and Gorelick, 1980; Frye, 1980; Gold and Byck, 1979; Guillemin, 1978; Harrison, 1981; Snyder, 1979). Naloxone, which is a natural antagonist to morphine and other narcotics, is administered to heroin addicts and others who overdose on narcotics to reverse respiratory depression. When naloxone is administered to someone not using exogenous narcotics, the antagonist acts to displace the natural endorphins and withdrawal symptoms may result. One method frequently employed in psychopharmacological research is to administer naloxone and observe which behaviors are affected; it is presumed that effects thereby observed are related to the function of our natural endogenous narcotics. Such research has concluded, for example, that endorphins are not involved in male or female sexual arousal; that they are involved in stress-induced eating; that either too high or too low a level of endorphins may play a role in mental disorders such as schizophrenia; and that certain exercises, particularly marathon running, raises our endorphin levels (Carr and Bullen, 1981; Ambinder and Schuster, 1979; Snyder, 1979). It is believed that, like external narcotics (e.g., morphine or heroin), endorphins have profound effects on mood and behaviors, only some of which are currently understood.

THE CRITICAL PARADIGM

As for the implications of endorphins for critical criminology and for humanistic sociology, one argument to consider goes something like this: We are a society filled with justified fears and anxieties about the tremendous number of violent crimes and property crimes that are "drug-related"—specifically, that are committed in part to support narcotic addicts' habits. Yet the use of narcotics by persons or the addiction of some man or woman to heroin is something that differs *merely in quantity, not in quality,* from the *natural* state of narcotic addiction in which *every one of us is addicted to our endorphins,* which are chemically nearly the same as morphine. Therefore: Is it not irrational to take a punitive approach toward heroin addiction and toward heroin addicts when their habit differs only in quantity and not in quality from everyone else's habit of endorphin (narcotic) addiction? It is most germane in this regard to note that medical research has shown that both the causal process leading to narcotic addiction and the ways out of exogenous narcotic addiction are closely related to that person's endorphin levels. That is, if everyone were to receive a shot of pure morphine sulfate, 10 mg., some would feel "high" and euphoric; others might feel scared or drowsy; others would perhaps feel nothing. Those who would feel especially good are likely to be those who *start out* with a naturally low level, comparatively speaking, of endorphins. Those starting out with a naturally high level, such as a marathon runner right after completing a race, would probably feel little or no effect from the morphine injection, since he or she would already be so loaded with natural morphine that the external source would produce minimal change in affective feelings.

Remembering that the current state of the art of medical knowledge concerning which factors lead to low or to high levels of naturally occurring brain opiates is extremely limited, it is quite plausible (and consistent with the available pharmacological data) to speculate that factors such as emotional stress brought about by economic poverty (and the resultant poor nutrition) could lead in a causal process to depleted levels of endorphin. Someone who has undergone these stresses and suffers from a depleted endorphin level would feel great when he or she first "shoots up" with heroin or morphine. Such an individual is likely to desire a continuation of this habit, which eventually evolves into an addiction. On the opposite end of the causal spectrum, when a narcotic addict attempts to withdraw from the use of exogenous narcotic substances, it has been demonstrated that natural beta-endorphin can replace the exogenous narcotics and prevent any withdrawal symptoms. That is, you could give someone infusions of beta-endorphin to make up for the *quantitative* deficiency in total narcotic levels as compared with the time period in which the individual was receiving external narcotics, in addition to the natural endorphin levels.

One may deduce that this psychopharmacological evidence cannot be ignored by anyone concerned with the phenomenon and problem of narcotic usage and addiction, or the crime trends which may result therefrom. In the endorphin research, we have found the key to increasing our understanding of the mechanisms involved in narcotic usage and addiction. In so doing, we also raise and confront profound challenges for criminal law, for the judiciary, for criminal sociologists, and for humanists. One illustration of this challenge, mentioned briefly already, may be particularly intriguing.

As noted earlier, the Controlled Substances Act of 1970 is the piece of federal legislation that regulates the use of narcotic drugs in the United States, as well as addressing the regulation of nonnarcotic controlled drugs, such as marijuana, cocaine, methaqualone, and LSD. It may be noted that, so far as we know, none of those drugs just referred to has any natural endogenous counterparts in humans, so that the kind of issue with regard to endorphins and exogenous narcotics that has been raised here has no application to these other nonnarcotic drugs or, for that matter, to alcohol; it is, though, believed that endorphins and other neurotransmitters may play a role in psychological and/or physical dependence on nonnarcotic drugs (and even dependence on some types of foods) through the production of something known as *exorphins*. My focus here, however, remains on endorphins and their implications for our current societal views (as reflected in our criminal laws) governing narcotic usage. The dilemma regarding endorphins becomes dramatic with the recognition that several major pharmaceutical firms are planning to market synthetic beta-endorphin in pill and injectable forms as analgesics (Snyder, 1979). The pertinent inquiry to the FDA and to the DEA, as well as for the courts, is: How will endorphins be classified according to the Controlled Substances Act? If they are classified as a strictly controlled drug (either in Schedule I or II), such as is currently the case with heroin and morphine, respectively, then the logic is evident. Endorphins are indeed morphine's endogenous counterpart and namesake. But then, are persons going to be arrested and prosecuted for felonious possession and usage (or sale) of endorphins—a substance human beings carry in their bodies at all times? Certainly not everyone can be arrested for possession or sale of endorphins; presumably those doing the arresting would themselves be in possession of endorphins. If during a blood transfusion some endorphins are transferred from one person to another, is this sale of a controlled substance? Though these examples sound absurd, consider the implications of the alternative scheme in which endorphins are not strictly regulated narcotic substances. If the FDA and the DEA decide to treat endorphin supplements in pill form as they now treat vitamins—reasonable, since we would nearly always only be taking endorphins to supplement our natural production of it—then endorphins could be sold over the counter. If this course of action is followed, what about morphine and heroin and opium? These substances, nearly identical to endorphins, again present the rational dilemma. How could society, through its legal authorities, continue to prosecute people in serious felony cases for selling synthetic heroin when synthetic endorphin would be sold over the counter and produce virtually identical physiological results—assuming the pure quality, that is, of both substances? To continue such prosecutions would violate principles of humanity and of common sense. While this has never prevented the imposition of irrational governmental policies in the past, we should not advocate the continuation of clearly counterproductive social or legal policy. Therefore, while past arguments for the legalization of narcotics have focused on several persuasive economic, pragmatic, and social realities, this exploration leads us into psychopharmacological conclusions which demand, and deserve, closer scrutiny.

FUTURE DIRECTIONS

A humanist sociologist or critical criminologist must be concerned with the human condition. In modern times the use of narcotics and all the consequences of such use—be they social, medical, economic, or legal—are very much a part of the human condition in the United States. If we address the evidence regarding endorphins in the right manner, it will enhance the humanistic and nonpunitive approach toward narcotic addiction and serve to reify our concerns for social justice. One may reasonably believe that there is great excitement and relevance to be gleaned from following through on this type of scientific data. But some other points must simultaneously be kept in mind. One of these is that there is a tremendous amount of money being made (and expended) in this country in the business of narcotic drugs. Billions of illegal dollars are implicated in the acquisition and sale of substances such as heroin, and many people's lives are damaged or ended as a result of the narcotics business. Consequently, it would be a mistake to draw the lesson from the psychopharmacological evidence simply that narcotics, because they are natural, are therefore healthy and fine substances. Rather, I would want to emphasize that the societal and legal approach to narcotic usage is today irrational and shortsighted. It is overly punitive and ignores major factors in humanism and in economics; it also overlooks, partly by intention and partly by neglect, that there are major political and economic power groups which benefit from the status quo of drug *misuse*. The endorphin evidence is germane *both* to alerting critical criminologists to the importance of looking at the biological factors in the causal processes of social problems and in building momentum to develop an approach that is more rational, less punitive, and will remove both the human suffering and the massive profits from the current state of narcotic usage, sale and addiction practices.

I believe that all glaringly neglected areas of criminology—including high-level or white-collar criminality and, in the present instance, sociobiology—have lots of dangers and imperfections inherent in a scholarly exploration of them. But these complex and problematic issues cannot be dismissed out of hand. To do so—particularly for critical criminologists—is to cut ourselves off and leave the humanistic perspective out in the cold while the social control theories march right along, and their advocates prosper with government research grants. That is not an acceptable scenario. To counteract it, modern critical theory in criminology must not suffer from a blind spot regarding sociobiology. So far, the blind spot is there.

REFERENCES

AMBINDER, R., and M. SCHUSTER (1979) "Endorphins: new gut peptides with a familiar face." Gastroenterology 77: 1132-1140.

BLACKWELL, B. (1979) "Current psychiatric research: the endorphins." Psychiatric Opinion 16: 9.

BLOOM, F. (1981) "Neuropeptides." Scientific American (November): 148-168.

——— and D. SEGAL (1976) "Endorphins: profound behavioral effects in rats suggest new etiological factors in mental illness." Science 194: 630-632.

BROCCARDO, D. (1981) "Pharmacological data on dermorphins, a new class of potent opioid peptides from amphibian skin." British J. of Pharmacology 73: 625.

BUNNEY, W., C. PERT, and W. KLEE (1979) "Basic and clinical studies of endorphins." Annals of Internal Medicine 91: 239-250.

BURGER, W. (1967) "The law and medical advances." Annals of Internal Medicine 78: 7-17.

CARR, D., and B. BULLEN (1981) "Physical conditioning facilitates the exercise-induced secretion of beta-endorphin and beta-lipotropin in women." New England J. of Medicine 305: 560.

CATLIN, D. and D. GORELICK (1980) "Clinical effects of beta-endorphin infusions," pp. 465-472 in Advances in Biochemical Psychopharmacology, Vol. 22. New York: Raven Press.

CONKLIN, J. (1975) The Impact of Crime. New York: Macmillan.

COMMENT (1973) "Criminal responsibility and the drug dependence defense—a need for judicial clarification." Fordham Law Rev. 42: 361-368.

FRYE, R. (1980) "The sociobiological paradigm: a new approach to drug-using behavior." J. of Psychedelic Drugs 12: 21-25.

GOLD, M. and R. BYCK (1979) "Endorphin locus-coeruleus connection mediates opiate action and withdrawal." Biomedicine 30: 1-4.

GOLD, M. and H. KLEBER (1979) "A rationale for opiate withdrawal symptomatology." Drug and Alcohol Dependence 4: 419-424.

GOLDSTEIN, A. (1976) "Opioid peptides (endorphins) in pituitary and brain." Science 193: 1081-1086.

GORDON, D. (1973) "Capitalism, class, and crime in America." Crime and Delinquency 19: 163-186.

GUILLEMIN, R. (1978) "Beta-lipotropin and endorphins: implications of current knowledge." Hospital Practice (November): 53-60.

HARRISON, J. (1981) "Endorphins and legal issues." J. of Legal Medicine 2, 4: 543-568.
——— (1978) "Some characteristics of young Israeli drug users." Drug Forum: J. of Human Issues 7: 167-172.

KRAMER, J. (1980) "The opiates: two centuries of scientific study." J. of Psychedelic Drugs 12: 89-103.

OLSON, R., A. KASTIN, and G. OLSON (1980) "Behavioral effects after systemic injection of opiate peptides." Psychoneuroendocrinology 5: 47-52.

PARGMAN, D. and M. BAKER (1980) "Running high: enkephalin indicted." J. of Drug Issues 10: 341.

SHOHAM, S. (1979) Salvation Through the Gutters: Deviance and Transcendence. New York: Hemisphere.

SNYDER, S. (1979) "Clinical relevance of opiate receptor and opioid peptide research." Nature 279: 13-14.

STEIN, L. and J. BELLUZZI (1978) "Brain endorphins and the sense of well-being: a psychobiological hypothesis," in Advances in Biochemical Psychopharmacology, Vol. 18. New York: Raven Press.

STOELTING, R. (1980) "Opiate receptors and endorphins: their role in anesthesiology." Anesthesia and Analgesia 59: 874-880.

SU, C. and C. LIN (1980) "Suppression of morphine abstinence in heroin addicts by beta-endorphin," in Advances in Biochemical Psychopharmacology, Vol. 22. New York: Raven Press.

TAYLOR, I., P. WALTON, and J. YOUNG (1975) Critical Criminology. London: Routledge & Kegan Paul.

TAYLOR, R. (1970) Good and Evil: A New Direction. New York: Macmillan.

THIO, A. (1979) Deviant Behavior. Boston: Houghton Mifflin.

USDIN, E., W. BUNNEY, and N. KLINE (1979) Endorphins in Mental Health Research. New York: Oxford Univ. Press.

WEIL, A. (1980) The Marriage of the Sun and Moon: A Quest for Unity in Consciousness. Boston: Houghton Mifflin.

IV

NEW DIRECTIONS—FROM THE SPECIFIC TO THE GENERAL

Norman K. Denzin

University of Illinois, Urbana

7

NOTES ON CRIMINOLOGY
AND CRIMINALITY

My intentions in this chapter are as follows: (1) briefly to call attention to the work of Michel Foucault and to suggest its implications for the study of power in the field of criminology; (2) to speak briefly to the criminogenic hypothesis as it has recently been reformulated to apply to the study of organizational crime (Farberman, 1975); (3) to reconsider the place of power, knowledge, and knowledge structures in the scientific disciplines; and (4) to suggest that criminologists must begin to study the embodied, built-up, situated character of criminal activity, as the activity occurs in the arenas of the natural social world. I will illustrate this fourth point through a discussion of Raskolnikov's act of murder in Fyodor Dostoyevsky's novel, *Crime and Punishment* (1866 [1950]).

POWER, KNOWLEDGE, AND CRIMINOLOGY

Discourse in the field of criminology contributes to the power-knowledge structure of a society that regularly produces legally defined criminal behavior (Foucault, 1980: 42). This discourse is indispensable to the functioning of society's penal agencies. It contributes to a tech-

AUTHOR'S NOTE: A version of this chapter was prepared for presentation at the 33rd Annual Meetings of the American Society of Criminology, Washington, D.C., November 1981. A great deal of the paper was worked out in conversations with Johanna K. Denzin and Richarad Herbert Howe, especially the discussion of Raskolnikov's crime.

nology of disciplinary reform that focuses criminological study on the offender, on criminogenic environments, and on the legal structures and practices that define and produce shifting rates in criminal behavior.

Recently a shift in focus to the level of organizational crime has occurred (see Geis, 1973; Ermann and Lundman, 1978a, 1978b; Roebuck and Weeber, 1978; Turk, 1980; Gross, 1978; Cressey, 1969; Clinard, 1950, 1979; Quinney, 1977; Chambliss, 1976; Sutherland, 1949). This research, guided by a version of the "criminogenic" hypothesis, argues that built into the very structure of organizations is an inherent inducement for the organization itself to engage in crime (Gross, 1978: 56). The criminogenic hypothesis, an expansion on the earlier thesis that criminal conduct is somehow a part of the personal makeup of particular classes or groups of individuals, or in some fashion flows from "high" criminogenic environments, introduces an economic element into crime's study, suggesting that crime is financially rewarding and not just confined to persons in the lower layers of the social structure. Indeed, the new criminology attempts the analysis and understanding of crime and deviance in terms of the legal codes and systems of economic production and organization that characterize a society. (See Sutherland, 1949, for a not so new formulation of this position.)

Bribery, kickbacks, antitrust violations, payoffs, fraud, and the circumvention of legal codes, all crimes against property, simply add to the criminologist's expanding taxonomy of crimes that may be studied. (But see Benson, 1981, for a reformulation of this problem.) And studies go on. The field of criminology has yet fully and directly to address the place, meaning, and character of criminal conduct within the social structures that make up today's societies.

If criminal conduct flows from the actions of individuals, from organizations and their representatives, from governmental agencies, and if entire national states can be judged to have engaged in criminal conduct, then where does the phenomenon of crime and its study find its locus? *Criminal activity arises from and out of the actions of interacting individuals, who, in the course of their dealings with one another, alter and modify the power relations they have with one another.* These alterations often require for their execution violations of legal codes and statutes.

However, a criminology strictly attached to the examination of violations of legal codes and statutes will fail to grasp the micropower relations in everyday life that underlie the basis of phenomena commonly termed "criminal" in nature and intent.

Michel Foucault (1977 [1980]) reminds the sociologist that power and micropower relations permeate every structure of a society. The anatomy of power in today's social structures reveals that it is not to be identified with the state, with its central apparatuses, or with its legal codes and control agencies. Power has no essence, no central place of location within social structure. Rather, it is to be found in the endless duplicating and replicating micropower relations and networks of inter-action that find their locus in factories, production plants, housing complexes, shops, hotels, neighborhood parks, streets, family homes, universities, hospitals, market centers, government offices, prison cells, retirement homes, professional associations, schools of law, board-rooms of corporations, floors of stock exchanges, and in the other social worlds that make up the everyday, taken-for-granted life worlds that persons routinely and not so routinely find themselves inhabiting and thrown into.

Criminology is nothing if not the study of the political anatomy of a society. For crime, phenomenologically understood, is a mode of action in the life world that is constructed and shaped by the micropower rela-tions that flow from a society's structures of interaction, power, and knowledge.

By confining their studies to legally defined categories of criminal behavior, criminologists have simply contributed to the social vocabu-lary of social control that today's societies appear to require if power is to be productive and not just repressive.[1] (Penal and judicial reforms, which stem from the legislative reforms of the eighteenth and nineteenth centuries, aim to return criminals to society as productive participants in the labor force. Criminologists have contributed to this enterprise through their focus on the criminal, on criminal environments, and on prisons as agencies of social, moral, and educational reform and con-trol.)

An anatomy of power, Nietzsche and Foucault suggest, reveal its location in the human body and in the body's embodied actions. Power, then, is not to be lodged in organizations, in environments, or in organi-zations. The hold exercised by power over the body (Sheridan, 1980: 219) renders the body productive, and the possessor of the body, the person, now becomes a productive agent, subject to the microcontrol of the myriad of agencies and relationships that combine to make up what are termed societies. Investing power in the person and the body makes persons the prisoners of their own power. To this extent there is no need to control persons from the outside. They are trapped within their own subjectivity and have turned power inward upon themselves and the others with whom they interact. Persons are both prisoners and prisons (contained and containers). It is this dialectical relationship—power, its location in the person, and the oppositions that obtain between persons and the powers invested in them, as agents of their own actions—that criminologists must begin to study.

Criminological knowledge is not a neutral knowledge. Following Foucault, Sheridan (1980: 220) observes that knowledge "derives not from some subject of knowledge, but from the power relations that invest it. Knowledge cannot be neutral. All knowledge is political." Stripped of its pure status as pure knowledge of an uncontaminated subject, knowledge now becomes an instrument of social control. As Foucault (1980: 226) states, in commenting on the investigations of psychology, psychiatry, pedagogy, and criminology into the field of criminology, "another power, another knowledge." The political anatomy of power deprives the science of criminology of its privileged status of a neutral science.

What, then, should criminologists study? They should be studying the origins, distribution, production, and control of knowledge systems within and throughout social structures. They should be studying power and its situated embodiment in the ordinary and out-of-the-ordinary practices of interacting individuals.

An examination of embodied power and practices, as lodged in persons, is called for, as is a dissection of power's anatomy in everyday life. The criminologist should examine power and do closeup and systematic analyses of the ordinary and out-of-the-ordinary practices that alter the micropower and personal relations between persons and their agencies. The study of crime and criminal interaction involves the examination of the legitimate and illegitimate uses to which knowledge is put in sets of power relations. Knowledge is invested in power relationships. Criminologists should study those who seize power and knowledge and put it to their own uses and purposes and, in so doing, repress, punish, coerce, destroy, injure and murder one another. Criminology must be critical. A disinterested criminology, one which strives only to record shifts and trends in the rates of criminal activity, simply contributes to the existing knowledge-power structure of a society.

CRIMINOGENIC BEHAVIOR AND VIOLENCE

In a recently completed study of criminogenic factors in the American liquor industry, the following statement was made by a vice-president for marketing for a major American distilling firm:

> We break the laws every day. If you think I go to bed at night worrying about it, you're crazy. Everybody breaks the law. The liquor laws are insane anyway [Denzin, 1977: 919].[2]

The core of the "American Organizational Way of Life" (Bell, 1960) is criminogenic and demands detailed study. Clearly, a knowledge of legal structures and their manipulation is warranted. Consider the following two descriptions of extortion, also drawn from the field of liquor control:

> The state monopoly over liquor licensing has converted the right to drink into a source of political capital—cash and favors—which is exploited by state and city governments and their agents, the police, to assure compliance with their interests. Politicians exact enormous fees for selling and transferring lucrative licenses, and the police are obliged to maintain the efficacy of the system by harassing those who do not adhere and protecting those in favor.

> Former County Board Chairman ——————— was found guilty on two charges that he shook down tavern owners in exchange for issuing or renewing their liquor licenses. . . . ——————— has been accused of extorting $17,500 from [two tavern owners] in exchange for helping [each tavern owner] obtain a liquor license [quoted in Denzin, 1977: 917; excerpts taken from Rubenstein, 1973: 420, and Fisher, 1976].

The actions of exacting fees for selling and transferring liquor licenses, converting the right to drink to a source of political capital, harassing liquor license holders, shaking down tavern owners, and extorting fees are situated practices that while admittedly criminal and illegal in nature and intent, are more fundamentally exercises in the micropolitics of power and its use. Knowledge is invested in power relationships. The study of crime involves the examination of the legitimate and illegitimate uses to which knowledge is put in a particular set of power relationships.

Now consider the following description of an aggravated assault, given by a female offender in her mid-20s:

> We were partying one night in my rooms at the hotel where I lived and worked. Everybody there was a regular, except for this one dude who I had rented a room down the hall. He just kind of drifted in, and X said that he knew the dude, so it was cool. We were all drinking wine, taking pills and having a mellow time when I overheard this dude ask X who I was and saying that I was a bitch. I said, "Hey, who's the bitch you are talking about?" and he said "You're the bitch." I thought to myself, "What does this dude think he's doing coming to my party uninvited and then calling me a fucking bitch?" I said, "Don't you come to my party and call me a bitch?" He said, "You are a bitch; I was high and you short-changed me out of fucking $20 when I paid you for my room today." I said, "Man you are crazy." He said, "Don't try to slick me, bitch; I'm hip; I'm an ex-con; I know what's happening and X knows I'm good people, so don't try to run that game on me."
>
> My friends were having a good time. I felt good, and I didn't want to spoil the mood for any problems behind $20, so I thought that I'd just pacify the chump and give him a lousy $20 and end it. I said, "Look man, I didn't shortchange you out of any money today, but just to show my good heart, I'll give you $20; how about that?" He said, "Well, since you needed it so fucking bad that you had to try to run a game like that past me, then you can keep it, bitch." Then I thought that motherfucker was just messing with me. He was trying to make me out as a petty hustler and call me a bitch right in front of my friends. I said to myself, "Please, motherfucker, don't mess with me any more." I finally said, "Mister, I'm warning you, don't you fuck with me any more or I'll show you what a fucking bitch is." He just looked at me, laughed and said, "I haven't seen the bitch yet who could kick my ass."
>
> Then I told myself, "This man has got to go one way or another; I've just had enough of this mother fucker messing with me; I'm going to cut his dirty motherfucking throat." I went into my bedroom, got a $20 bill and my razor. I said to myself, "The motherfucker wouldn't stop fucking with me and now he's hung himself," and I walked out of the bedroom. I went up to him with a big smile on my face. I held the $20 bill in my hand out in front of me and hid the razor in my other hand. Then I sat on his lap and said, "O.K., you're a fast dude; here's your $20 back." He said, "I'm glad

you're finally admitting it." I looked at him with a smile and said, "Let me seal it with a kiss." I said to myself, "Motherfucker, now I'll show you what a fucking bitch is," and then I bent over like I was going to kiss him and started slicing up his throat" [Reported by Athens, 1980: 36-37].

While vice-presidents of distilling and importing companies break the laws everyday, and politicians engage in systematic extortion practices, this crime reported by Athens involves physical violence. It demonstrates power, physically enacted, put into play, and the elements of breaking a law are apparently suspended while the offender carries out the slicing up of another person's throat. Athens's study meets the symbolic interactionist requirement that "the study identify the way in which the actor sees and defines the situation in which he is placed and in which he comes to act violently" (Blumer, 1980: x). Conventional criminology too often takes the occurrence of criminal acts as a given without studying the acts themselves (Blumer, 1980: xi). As a consequence, a great deal of criminological research stands far removed from the actual buildup and occurrence of criminal activity. Criminologists need to redirect their attention to the natural social worlds of criminal activity. Such studies would examine the inner and outer trajectory of criminal acts and actions which result in violence, blackmail, extortion, bribery, tax evasion, embezzlement, and murder. (See, for example, those studies associated with the Chicago school of sociology in the 1930s, especially reviews of these studies by Thrasher, Lindesmith, Cressey, Shaw, Sutherland, Wirth, and Anderson and Becker).

A PHENOMENOLOGY OF MURDER

Fyodor Dostoyevesky, in his 1866 study of *Crime and Punishment,* offers the criminologist a thick phenomenological description of a murder. In the account given below, Raskolnikov is committing the perfect crime, a crime which to this point in the exposition has been an "It," "a simple fantasy," "a plaything of his mind," "only yesterday's thought in his mind," "an act still unnamed." But now he acts, as follows:

His hands were fearfully weak, he felt them every moment growing more numb and more wooden. He was afraid he would let the axe slip and fall. . . . . A sudden giddiness came over him.

"But what has he tied it up like this for?" the old woman cried with vexation and moved towards him.

He had not a minute more to lose. He pulled the axe quite out, swung it with both arms, scarcely conscious of himself, and almost without effort, almost mechanically, brought the blunt side down on her head. He seemed not to use his own strength in this. But as soon as he had once brought the axe down, his strength returned.

The old woman was always bareheaded. Her thin, light hair, streaked with grey, thickly smeared with grease, was plaited in a rat's tail and fastened by a broken horn comb which stood out on the nape of her neck. As she was so short, the blow fell on the very top of her skull. She cried out, but very faintly, and suddenly sank all of a heap on the floor, raising her hands to her head. In one hand she still held "the pledge." Then he dealt her another and another blow with the blunt side and on the same spot. The blood gushed as from an overturned glass, the body fell back. He stepped back, let it fall, and at once bent over her face; she was dead. Her eyes seemed to be staring out of their sockets, the brow and the whole face were drawn and contorted convulsively.

He laid the axe on the ground near the dead body and felt at once in her pocket (trying to avoid the streaming body)—the same right hand pocket from which she had taken the key on his last visit. He was in full possession of his faculties, free from confusion or giddiness, but his hands were still trembling. He remembered afterwards that he had been particularly collected and careful, trying all the time not to get smeared with blood [Dostoyevsky, 1950: 71].

THE HERMENEUTICS OF CRIME

Criminal situations may be studied hermeneutically (Heidegger, 1962: 232)—that is, in terms of the prior understandings and interpretations criminals, victims, and criminologists bring to the situations of criminal conduct. (Heidegger suggests that all situations are approached with a sense of foresight, forehaving, or foreunderstanding, and foreconceptions or prior pictures of the situation.) The interpretation of a criminal act involves the grasping of what was understood about the situation as one entered into it. An understanding of a sequence of criminal activity involves the appropriation of the totality of that which has been interpreted *once the act has been dissected and taken apart.* A circle of interpretation occurs, for what was known about the activity before it occurred enters into the organization of the activity and shapes the subsequent accomplishments, interpretations, and understandings of the conduct.

The hermeneutical understanding of criminal activity resolves into a series of steps. First, an understanding of the foreinterpretations and understandings of the criminal (and the victim) toward one another must be related. In Raskolnikov's crime Lizavota Ivanovna is described, in the words of a student, as "stupid," "senseless," "worthless," "spiteful," "ailing," as a person "who will die in a day or two" (p. 60). Further, if she were killed, "a 1,000 good deeds could be done." In his prior dealings with her, Lizavota was seen as cheating him, as demeaning him, as not respecting him.

The interpretation of the foreunderstandings held by the criminal will also involve dissection and laying out of the meanings, motives, understandings, images, and accounts held by the criminal prior to and during the occurrence of the criminal act. Raskolnikov saw himself planning and executing the perfect crime. There would be no witnesses, no evidence left behind, no motive that would link him to the crime. The reader learns, after the crime has been committed, that Raskolnikov has written a philosophical article justifying the crime of murder for persons of superior intellect, if the act could be justified in terms of its consequences for humanity. This account was part of his justification for the murder. Further, as just noted, he saw the old lady as despicable and of no human worth.

This kind of analysis applies even if the relationship is one of seriality (Sartre, 1976) or unrelatedness. The victim may be a member (in the mind of the criminal) of a nameless collectivity that stands in opposition to the criminal's life world.

Raskolnikov stood in a financially subordinate relationship to the old lady, yet he regarded himself as morally and intellectually her superior. Having denied her worth, his destruction of her affirmed his moral sense of superiority and sense of being.

The second step in the hermeneutical understanding of criminal activity requires that the doing of the act be understood and *temporally displayed* as a practical accomplishment, having the characteristics of articulated movements through time and space ending in the actual doing of the crime. To the point of its accomplishment, the crime will exist in the criminal's mind as a vague, yet recognizable "It" that has yet to be done. Criminal acts, like all human acts, are recognized as "Its," as things or a thing, or an act to be done, before "It" is done. However, once recognized as an accomplishment, once done, "It" is typically named and identified (if criminal) within a legal language and vocabulary. Once accomplished, the act is often claimed as belonging to the person, and in many cases this named and possessed act may be all that the person has, or is all that the person can call his or her own (see Abbott, 1980).

In Raskolnikov's crime, up to the murder, the act is referred to: "it is not serious at all" (p. 2). "It's simply a fantasy to amuse myself." However, as he approaches the actual doing of the crime, it becomes: "Besides it was not only yesterday's thought. . . . It has taken a new meaning and quite unfamiliar shape" (p. 42). By page 49, he can see himself as having done the crime. He states: "I shall go to Razumihins of course, but not now, I shall go to him . . . on the day after It." Here, in the middle of the sentence, for the first time, Dostoyevsky capitalizes "It." As Garfinkel et al. (1981: 157-158), following Harvey Sacks, observe, "this 'It' has a vagueness that is identical with it. It has a definiteness of sense, of reference, before it is produced."[3]

The actual murder found Raskolnikov barely conscious of his own body. His hands were weak, he was afraid he would drop the axe. "Almost mechanically [he] brought the blunt side down on her head." He "seemed not to use his own strength . . . but as soon as he had brought the axe down, his strength returned." "He remembered afterwards that he had been particularly careful and collected."

Third, as movements toward accomplished "Its," criminal acts have the characteristics of embodied, situated practices and must be so understood. Once identified as falling within the domain of criminological studies, these acts should be approached as normal activities, practices, and projects.

The interpretive, embodied practices sociologists examine have a core of recurring activities that must be learned, traced out, rehearsed, taught, coached, felt, expressed, interpreted, and practiced. These practices in the company of others become social productions. These practices and their productions constitute reality as it is known, felt, and experienced by interacting individuals.

Embodied practices, to summarize, have the following elements: (1) They consist of ongoing streams of action and activity, both verbal and nonverbal; (2) as streams of action, they cluster into ensembles of moving activity; (3) they have emergent, unfinished features, even those that are planned; (4) they are interactive, involving the presence and ensembled activity of one or more persons (dyads, triads, groups) in their accomplishments; (5) they are situated, locked into situations, and part of the situations in which they evolve; (6) they have inner and outer components, and they move through the phenomenological and interactive streams of the person (Denzin, 1980: 255); (7) they are owned and claimed by the person; (8) they have the essential characteristic of evolving accomplishments which can only be understood while they are being produced; and (9) they are temporal accomplishments, requiring movements through time and space. They are, in this respect, invisible structures of action, which are written in the movements of the person. These invisible, nontraceable, nonretrievable structures of action are visible to the doer of the action and to the observer, yet their traces are written in movements through the air.

In Raskolnikov's production, he carries himself with haste to the old lady's rooms. His actions are an ensemble of flowing, moving activity. Halfway to her flat he remembers that he had forgotten to buy a hat to wear. As he leaves his rooms, the emergent problem of securing the axe arises and he must make a quick judgment on how to remove the axe from the landlady's rooms. His murder is interactive, for he must engage the old woman in a conversation and draw her into a field of activity that will permit the murder to occur. The murder itself is situated in the outer room of her flat. Phenomenologically, as he brings the axe down against her head, he was "scarcely conscious of himself." This murder, once done, is his, and in his own mind he claims the perfect crime as his. However, and very soon, he begins to dissociate himself from the crime, at times treating it as a dream. Still, he acts in a sequence, dealing "another and another blow with the blunt side and on the same spot." The murder, then, was a temporal production which could only be recognized as he was doing it.

Unaware of the movements of his arms, he saw only that the axe smashed her head. The "streaming body" with "her eyes staring out of their sockets," the "blood" served merely as evidence that "It" was a "murder" accomplished when "He laid the axe on the ground near the dead body." Any inner doubt he may have had about his ability to carry out the perfect crime was at this moment no longer relevant.

Fourth, the moral and consequential foreinterpretations of the criminal act must be articulated, for it is these interpretations that may prevent crime. Unlike the organization of other activities, the foreinterpretations of a criminal or deviant act require a neutralization and redefinition of the self in relationship to the *personalized moral and legal meanings* that bound the act as it is formed in the person's mind. The act must be seen as one the person is capable of doing. Phenomenologically, the act has become a personal act, removed from the boundaries of exterior constraints and standards.

Not only is the act given special interpretations, but so is the victim. In this sense, criminal activity is a dialectical confrontation with the routine, mundane, yet sacred premises and presences of others (Heidegger, 1962: 163). Criminal conduct against persons or their properties diminishes the other's presence in the world and devalues the person and his or her possessions (Scheler, 1913 [1962]. Moral judgments underlie criminal conduct.

In an often implicit moral comparison between the criminal and the victim, the victim is transformed into an object warranting wrath, deception, destruction, vengeance, and even annihilation (Sykes and Matza, 1959). Real or potential victims have brought this fate on themselves. In Raskolnikov's crime, as noted above, the pawnbroker was "stupid," "senseless," "worthless," "spiteful," "ailing" and injurious to Raskolnikov.

For the woman reported on by Athens, the victim has "messed with her" long enough. He "wouldn't stop fucking with me and now he's hung himself." The victim may call out the crime in the criminal, a theme pursued with insight by Simenon, the French novelist.[4] The victim, or the victims, are considered the causes of the person's present situation. A causal delusion, or perception, underlies and becomes a precondition for the organization of the criminal act. Accompanying this delusion, or reinterpretation of the other, is a "neutralization" of the consequences and meanings of one's acts (Sykes and Matza, 1959).

Whether animated from resentment (Scheler, 1962), alienation, despair, delerium, disorganization, pleasure seeking, confusion, or deliberate and calculated, criminal interaction represents built-up activity that changes and alters its course as it is produced. Lodged in situations, embedded in ongoing patterns of activity, criminal conduct assumes a recognizable shape as it is accomplished. Such activities have constructed, halting, often hesitating elements. Frequently, the criminal recognizes the doing of a criminal act only after it has been completed and given retrospective meaning. In and during the act, the person may stand in a suspended, nearly disembodied relationship to the conduct.

Partly because the person is often suspended from and outside his or her criminal doings (it's not me doing this), an unfinished quality may linger after the act, as for instance in the realization that it could have been done differently, or that there were messy incriminating details and facts left behind.

Up into his actual ringing of the old lady's doorbell, Raskolnikov did not think he could go through with the act. He was still hesitating when she did not immediately answer the door. He was trembling as she opened it.

As the act is being contemplated, the person may, perhaps only momentarily, consider that the act which is being formulated carries possibilities of apprehension and of being placed within a new arena of meaning and self-understanding. Insofar as commission of the act will be denied, a subtle movement must occur: to view oneself as distinct from what one has been. As with Raskolnikov, thought thus, to act so to speak, has been accomplished. Paradoxically, it only remains to do what has been done.[5]

Such thoughts give the criminal act an inner side and inner life of its own. It has the features of a private or invisible act which will remain so if the person is not apprehended. After all, the thinker of the thoughts was not apprehended during the thinking of the thoughts that bounded the act prior to its doing.

It now remains for the person to act. When the act occurs, persons may suspend themselves, indeed be unable to report on the circumstances of their action. (This will be especially the case if the activity is chemically influenced.)

Fifth, the constructions and reconstructions of understandings which emerge after the act has been completed, named, and claimed can be understood and grasped. Here the meanings of the act to the victim, the criminal, and the criminologist can be fitted into an articulated structural totality, unlike many victimization and criminal career studies, which leave out the interactive-interpretive relationship and meanings that obtain between the criminal and the victim.

In Raskolnikov's crime, redemption was sought after he had endured his own self-inflicted punishment. His light sentence flowed from his actions after the crime. He never spent the money that was stolen, nor did he pawn the objects that were taken. These were interpreted as mitigating factors.

MEANING

Raskolnikov's crime can now be understood. He dared think what only a few people would think. Having the thought, he had no choice but to act. The thought—not alienation, frustration, deprivation or mental states commonly attached to social structures—set him apart from others. Raskolnikov acted to and for himself, not for others. How these thoughts are thought should occupy the criminologist.

CONCLUSIONS

Criminal acts are acts which alter existing power-knowledge relationships. They can be studied and understood hermeneutically as embodied, personal accomplishments. If one of the objects of criminology is to understand crime's place in society and social structures, then the close-up study of criminality in the manner suggested in this chapter seems warranted.

NOTES

1. The productive and repressive views and uses of power require elaboration. Until the middle of the nineteenth century Foucault argues that power was repressive in its organization, in the state, often in the form of the monarchy, applying power against the criminal. Execution of criminals represented the ultimate form of repressive power. Utilitarian theories of power and the state stood midway between pure retribution and rehabilitation. Utilitarian retribution punished the criminal in proportion to the severity of the crime. Rehabilitative theories of power and crime concern the making of offenders into productive members of society and assume that power is lodged inside the person. Offenders are punished for abuse of personal power, then rehabilitated. Power, as a productive resource inside the person, is a relatively recent development in the organization of post-industrial societies, or so Foucault argues.

2. The fact that this particular corporation employed a legal staff of considerable size perhaps contributes to this view of the law and the legal system.

3. On "It," see Garfinkel et al. (1981: 157-178), who take the term from Harvey Sacks's unpublished lectures. An "It" has a definiteness recognizability, and "understoodness," before "It" occurs through the accomplishments of the persons doing and making "It." After "It" has occurred, it is often named.

4. Richard Howe suggested, in this respect, the Maigret series by Simenon. Dashiell Hammett's five novels (*The Thin Man, The Glass Key, The Maltese Falcon, The Red Harvest,* and *The Dain Curse*) also explore this point, with a special emphasis on power, knowledge, and crime. Catherine A. Daubard suggested this point to me.

5. Harold Pepinsky has noted that some people, for example, claim blackout and fail to acknowledge commission of the act. These claims are suggestive of Sartre's (1939[1962]) observation that during extreme emotional experiences persons annihilate their consciousness in the face of a hostile, threatening world (pp. 89-90). This process of blanking out one's consciousness may represent a passive reaction to an environment that is perceived as extremely threatening. Fainting and extreme exhaustion after such acts are not uncommon. Raskolnikov returned to his home and slept after the murder. Upon awakening he feared that he had dreamt the act.

REFERENCES

ABBOTT, J. (1980) In the Belly of the Beast. New York: Knopf.

ANDERSON, N. (1923) The Hobo. Chicago: Univ. of Chicago Press.

ATHENS, L. H. (1980) Violent Criminal Acts and Actors: A Symbolic Interactionist Study. Boston: Routledge & Kegan Paul.

BECKER, H. S. (1966) "Introduction," pp. v-xviii in C. R. Shaw, The Jack-Roller. Chicago: Univ. of Chicago Press.

BELL, D. (1960) The End of Ideology: On the Exhaustion of Political Ideas in the Fifties. New York: Free Press.

BENSON, M. (1981) "Collateral consequences of conviction for a white collar crime." Ph.D. dissertation, University of Illinois, Urbana.

BLUMER, H. (1980) "Foreward," pp. ix-xii in L. H. Athens, Violent Criminal Acts and Actors. Boston: Routledge & Kegan Paul.

CHAMBLISS, W. J. (1976) "Functional and conflict theories of crime," in W. J. Chambliss and M. Mankoff (eds.) Whose Law? What Order? New York: John Wiley.

CLINARD, M. B. (1950) The Black Market. New York: Holt, Rinehart & Winston.

———— and P. C. YEAGER (1979) "Corporate crime: issues in research," pp. 155-172 in E. Sagarin (ed.) Criminology: New Concerns. Beverly Hills, CA: Sage.

CRESSEY, D. R. (1969) Theft of the Nation: The Structure and Operations of Organized Crime in America. New York: Harper & Row.

DENZIN, N. K. (1980) "A phenomenology of emotion and deviance." Zeitschrift fur Soziologie, Jg. 9, Heft 3, Juli 1980, S. 251-261.

———— "Notes on the criminogenic hypothesis: a case study of the American liquor industry." Amer. Soc. Rev. 42: 905-920.

DOSTOYEVSKY, F. (1950) Crime and Punishment (1866). New York: Vintage.

ERMANN, M. D. and R. J. LUNDMAN (1978a) "Deviant acts by complex organizations: deviance and social control at the organizational level of analysis," Soc. Q. 29: 55:67.

———— (1978b) Corporate and Governmental Deviance: Problems of Organizational Behavior in Contemporary Society. New York: Oxford Univ. Press.

FARBERMAN, H. (1975) "A criminogenic market structure: the automobile industry." Soc. Q. 16: 438-457.

FISHER, D. D. (1976) "Coles found guilty of tavern owner shakedowns." Chicago Sun-Times, March 27, p. 8.

FOUCAULT, M. (1980) Power and Knowledge. New York: Pantheon.

———— (1977) Discipline and Punish. New York: Pantheon.

GARFINKEL, H., M. LYNCH, and E. LIVINGSTON (1981) "The work of a discovering science construed with materials from the optically discovered pulsar." Philosophy of the Social Sciences 11: 131-158.

GEIS, G. (1973) "Deterring corporate crime," pp. 246-258 in R. Nader and M. Green (eds.) Corporate Power in America. New York: Viking.

GROSS E. (1978) "Organizational crime: a theoretical perspective," pp. 55-85 in N. K. Denzin (ed.) Studies in Symbolic Interaction, Vol. I. Greenwich, CT: JAI Press.

HEIDEGGER, M. (1982) The Basic Problems of Phenomenology. Bloomington: Indiana State Univ. Press.

———— (1962) Being and Time. New York: Harper & Row.

LINDESMITH, A. R. (1947) Opiate Addiction. Bloomington, IN: Principia Press.

QUINNEY, R. (1977) Class, State and Crime. New York: David McKay.

ROEBUCK, J. and S. WEEBER (1978) Political Crime in the United States: Analyzing Crime by and Against Government. New York: Praeger.

RUBENSTEIN, J. (1973) City Police. New York: Farrar, Straus and Girous.

SARTRE, J. P. (1976) Critique of Dialectical Reason. London: NLP.

——— (1962) Sketch for a Theory of the Emotions (1939). London: Methuen.

SCHELER, M. (1962) Ressentiment (1913). New York Free Press.

SHAW, C. R. (1931) The Natural History of a Delinquent Career. Chicago: Univ. of Chicago Press.

SHERIDAN, A. Michel Foucault: The Will to Truth. New York: Pantheon.

SUTHERLAND, E. (1949 White Collar Crime. New York: Dryden.

SYKES, G. M. and D. MATZA (1959) "Techniques of neutralization: a theory of delinquency." Amer. Soc. Rev. 22: 664-670.

TAYLOR, I., P. WALTON, and J. YOUNG (1973) The New Criminology: For a Social Theory of Deviance. London: Routledge & Kegan Paul.

THRASHER, F. (1963) The Gang. Chicago: Univ. of Chicago Press.

TURK, A. (1980) "Analyzing official deviance: for nonpartisan conflict analyses in criminology," pp. 78-91 in J. A. Inciardi (ed.) Radical Criminology: The Coming Crisis. Beverly Hills, CA: Sage.

WIRTH, L. (1929) The Ghetto. Chicago: Univ. of Chicago Press.

Henry N. Pontell

University of California, Irvine

8

SYSTEM CAPACITY AND CRIMINAL JUSTICE
Theoretical and Substantive Considerations

DETERRENCE AND THE CRIME RATE SYSTEM

Criminal deterrence continues to be a major goal of the American criminal justice system. Politicians and the public cling to the notion that increasing formal penalty structures will reduce crime. This belief undoubtedly contains a grain of truth. Under certain circumstances the threat of negative consequences will lead to the avoidance of proscribed behaviors. In situations involving crime and the law enforcement apparatus, however, this notion is highly problematic. Crime rates are a function of social structural, psychological, economic, and political factors as well as legal punishment.

When crime rates rise as a result of extralegal factors such as unemployment, the criminal justice system has but a limited capacity to respond. Today, as government resources decline, the popular imagery of law and its enforcement as a "lever" used to control the growth of crime becomes increasingly tenuous. The ability of punishment to deter crime depends, at least in part, on crime levels and the amount of work brought before the relatively resource-fixed criminal justice system.

This is particularly relevant in regard to concepts of "system capacity" (Pontell, 1978), "resource saturation" (Nagin, 1978), "system overload" (Geerken and Gove, 1977), and "crime rate system" (Henshel,

AUTHOR'S NOTE: I would like to thank Gilbert Geis and Paul Jesilow for their useful comments on an earlier draft of this chapter.

1978), all approaches which address the manipulation of the criminal sanctioning process. Environmental demands on organizational resources and the distribution of those resources in the criminal justice system may be largely responsible for what the system actually "produces" in terms of reported crime rates, arrests, convictions, and sentences (Pepinsky, 1980; Pontell, 1979).

Henshel (1978), for example, refers to the "crime rate system," which denotes the various relationships among crime rates and criminal justice practices. In describing the system capacity model, which views official sanctioning practices as dependent on levels of crime, and the deterrence model, which proposes that crime is a function of such sanctioning, Henshel notes: "the system capacity model . . . as well as the deterrence model . . . can both be seen for analytical purposes as components of a larger overall crime rate system, which describes the causal linkages between crime rate and various criminal justice practices" (1978: 44). Thus, the notion of a crime rate system provides a framework for studying the complex net of relations between crime and punishment practices. Moreover, it emphasizes the fact that crime may affect punishment just as much as, if not more than, punishment affects crime.

The system capacity model was developed to provide both a conceptual framework and a heuristic tool for examining the mitigating effects of crime on levels of punishment and, in turn, the likelihood of achieving general deterrence for felony crimes (see Pontell, 1978; Gibbs, 1978; Tittle, 1978; Henshel, 1978). The model does not question deterrence doctrine in theory but, rather, the ability of criminal justice institutions—especially the courts—to achieve it to any considerable degree in practice. It may be that deterrence can be accomplished for certain population subgroups without necessarily sanctioning with great certainty or severity (Toby, 1981), but this raises a totally different question concerning the "symbolic" nature of sanctions. The following discussion considers the notion of affecting general deterrence through "objective properties" of punishment, and attempts to integrate and highlight various perspectives that can be used in studying the system's capacity to generate and administer criminal sanctions. Substantive issues of system overcrowding and crime control policy will also be discussed.

The system capacity model of crime and punishment proposes that crime influences legal sanctioning more than sanctioning affects crime. Conditions formulated by the classical school of criminology for punishment to serve as a deterrent (e.g., certainty, celerity, and severity of sanctions) are generally not met under the current and past operation of criminal justice agencies. In discussing what he terms the "inherent difficulties in criminal justice," Pound (1975: 68-69) notes:

> It is hardly possible for any legal machinery to do all which our voluminous penal legislation expects of it . . . . Thus, there is constant pressure upon the law to "do something," whether it may do anything worthwhile or not.

Pound saw the difficulties in realizing formal goals of the law as a direct result of the social, cultural, and political milieu within which the law and the criminal justice system operate. Social change and increased modernization eroded familiar mechanisms of control and, at the same time, increased the demands on formal social control agencies which were then, and to a large degree remain, experimental in nature.

> This complete change in the background of social control involves much that may easily be attributed to ineffectiveness in criminal justice, and yet means only that it is called on to do the whole work, where once it shared its task with other agencies and was invoked, not for every occasion, but exceptionally [Pound, 1975: 14-15].

This statement remains as potent today as when it was put forth five decades ago. The inherent limitations of criminal justice and the law in producing social control results from the symbolic distance of law from the individual and from the amount of work the legal system must assume as informal social control mechanisms lose their force. Such limitations become more consequential as society develops, making formal goals of criminal justice and the law less attainable. That is, penological goals such as deterrence become harder to accomplish as limitations on the law intensify.

Pound's notion that there are structured limits to the legal system's capacity to reach formal goals is consistent with more recent analyses. Although there are widespread rational-legal rules of procedure and formally espoused goals of criminal justice, there is also widespread discretion for legal authorities, which in turn affects the system's capacity to mete out punishment. This aspect of law permits informal arrangements to arise, such as plea bargaining and other forms of cooperative production. Within such a system of interaction, which stresses norms of cooperation over more formal legal norms of conflict and adversariness, it seems plausible that penological considerations (including deterrence) will become secondary to administrative and personal goals of participants. As Feeley (1973) has noted, there may be no *goal* or *goals* of criminal justice in practice, but only formal goals in the strictly legal-traditional sense. Officials are generally concerned with crime prevention through general deterrence. This does not necessarily imply, however, that sanctioning activities will either reflect this formal goal of punishment or be effective in achieving it. As Eisenstein and Jacob (1977: 267) note: "The organizational structure of the courtroom workgroup guarantees that those who contribute to the sentencing decision have little concern for the fate of the defendant except in a few highly publicized cases."

SYSTEM CAPACITY AND CRIME CONTROL

Rates of punishment depend on the sanctioning capacity of the criminal justice system—especially the courts. Sanctioning capacity can be conceptualized as a function of many factors: (1) the structure of the law, especially procedural law; (2) the formal and informal organizational relationships both within and among criminal justice agencies; (3) the distribution of resources in the system; (4) the social, political, and cultural milieus within which the system exists; and (5) other external environmental constraints, including the volume of cases to be processed. In an overall sense, sanctioning capacity can be viewed as *the willingness and/or ability of the criminal justice system to enforce laws and mete out punishment.*

Whether or not punishment deters may be a moot question until we know more about the ecology of crime and punishment and the factors that affect the generation and administration of legal sanctions. While it is difficult, if not impossible, to determine precisely the overall capacity to arrest, convict, and sentence violators, certain aspects of the concept allow for empirical analysis. For example, the capacity of the judicial system to generate and administer sanctions depends largely on the relationship between resources and workload demands. Where resources are generous and demands light, sanctioning capacity is likely to be high. Conversely, sanctioning capacity would be low where resources are scarce and demands heavy.

An inverse relationship between crime and punishment may certainly be consistent with the notion that sanctions reduce crime. The same relationship can also be interpreted, however, as showing that low rates of crime *allow* the criminal justice system to be more punitive. This latter notion is more consistent with functionalist theories of deviance (e.g., Durkheim, 1966; Erikson, 1966), which view the maintenance of social boundaries through the redefinition of deviance as such deviance either becomes more prevalent or declines.

Pepinsky notes: "The findings of deterrence researchers—that the probability of sanction, and sometimes the severity of sanctions, increase as crime rates go down—is consistent with the idea that deterrence works better in areas that need less crime control in the first place" (1980: 131). Pepinsky posits that the less often an offense occurs, the better deterrence could operate. Put another way, deterrence theory, or "doctrine" (Gibbs, 1978), requires conditions such as certainty, severity, and celerity of punishment as well as respect and knowledge of law, which, if prevalent, make the use of deterrence largely unnecessary to begin with.

In addition, it seems unlikely that certainty and severity of punishment can be accomplished simultaneously (Galliher et al., 1973; Balbus, 1973). That is, it appears inevitable that they are inversely related given the resource constraints of criminal justice. This notion is consistent with the system capacity model, as courts and prisons cannot sustain long-term "crackdowns" which extend their organizational resources beyond practical and sometimes legal limits (Balbus, 1973). Thus, an inverse relationship between certainty and severity is due to structural limitations imposed by environmental demands (e.g., public demands for control, crime, and organizational caseloads) and the law itself.

In discussing the control of crime rates, Pepinsky notes (1980: 146) the paradoxical implications of system capacity for the criminal justice system.

> As citizens refer more problems than the police can handle, the more offense reports the police file, the worse the prognosis for arrest. But if police show that they are arresting suspects for a larger proportion of complaints, citizens are encouraged to report still more offenses. U.S. police arrest rates now indicate that:
>
> 1. Crime threatens to get worse.
> 2. Police are hard put just to keep arrests in proportion to crime.
> 3. Therefore, police need more support.
>
> Thus, increased support for officials feeds the cycle. More support carries the expectation of more arrests, which creates room for more offense reporting. This makes it harder to maintain clearance rates by arrest,

which implies a greater need to support police and other criminal justice officials.

Pepinsky's analysis is consistent with others which put forward the idea that police resources are just as likely to "produce" crime rates as to respond to them (Black, 1970; Pontell, 1979; Jacob and Rich, 1981). Such a condition would be more pronounced for police than for other criminal justice agencies, since the police are the most visible arm of the system and typically represent the "front line of defense" against crime. The most politically defensible actions for lawmakers usually entail increasing resources for police, perhaps at the expense of courts and prisons. This resource distribution has implications for generating and administering criminal punishments, since relative resource allocations for different criminal justice agencies help determine their respective organizational capacities for dealing with work inputs. Relatively high amounts of police resources compared to prosecutorial resources within a given jurisdiction, for example, would produce conditions favorable to court and prison overload and the subsequent diminution of sanctioning activity.

Actual levels of crime in conjunction with current laws, enforcement practices, and resources determine both the type and magnitude of work inputs of criminal justice agencies. Such inputs also reflect organizational exigencies and relationships (Reiss, 1971). This appears to be true at all levels of the criminal justice system. For example, when crime levels increase, police may be forced to pursue only the most serious crimes due to limited organizational resources, political demands for priority in controlling serious crime, and expectations as to subsequent prosecutorial and judicial decision making. Similarly, court officials who face increased caseloads may dismiss more cases, reduce charges, and impose lighter sentences. While the notion that plea bargaining would increase under such circumstances is still under debate in the literature (Feeley, 1973; Heumann, 1975, 1978; Nardulli, 1979), informal penalty structures ("going rates") used to bargain cases may be reduced to accommodate increasing caseloads. Even the use of such "safety-valve institutions," however, may not offset the increased demand placed on organizational resources.

Perhaps the most obvious results of strain in the system are found in the current conditions in state prisons and local jails. Overcrowded prisons, which are relatively invisible to the public eye (except when they are temporarily brought to the forefront by a major disturbance), require increased use of parole and release of prisoners when the harshness of prison conditions exceeds "acceptable" legal limits. States currently are facing federal orders to reduce prison populations in facilities that have been judged (sometimes reluctantly) to be in violation of constitutional guidelines. In a recent case involving the Indiana State Prison at Michigan City, for example, a federal judge found: "In the context of the physical plant and the limits on staffing, this overcrowding constitutes a violation of the Eighth Amendment of the Constitution of the United States" (Carroll, 1981). It should be noted that this case was not initiated through official channels, but was a result of a class-action lawsuit by inmates who claimed that the overcrowding constituted "cruel and unusual punishment."

Such situations are likely to increase as growth rates in prisons climb, especially in states with high crime levels. From a theoretical standpoint, overcrowded prisons document the criminal justice system's limited capacity to respond to the crime problem through conventional means.

STRUCTURAL AND INSTITUTIONAL LIMITATIONS TO SANCTIONING

Limits to crime control are present for all offenses but manifest themselves in the case of white-collar crime particularly clearly. Katz (1980) views the institutional capacity to investigate and prosecute such crimes as a function of practical resource limitations, given the overall responsibilities of the prosecutor's office and existing institutional arrangements. Resources and institutional arrangements are in turn affected both by the laws governing the control of white-collar crime and the political milieu within which such laws are enforced and resources distributed. In documenting the increased role of federal prosecutors in proceeding against white-collar offenders, Katz (1980: 175) notes:

In a sense, the most serious crimes are those which attempt to make use of politically powerful or economically elite positions to frustrate detection and prosecution; white-collar crimes define the boundaries of the criminal justice system's capacities and the limits of moral integrity in the economy and polity.

Katz views the relationship between institutional capacity and the social environment as determining the strength of efforts to investigate, prosecute, and punish white-collar crime. Thus, as in the case of

common crime, efforts to control white-collar crime will be affected by
the organizational environment and the institutional capacity of
criminal justice agencies. In addition, given relatively fixed resources,
the higher the demand for the control of common crime, the lower the
system's capacity to investigate and prosecute white-collar offenses. The
system must accommodate the "most serious" cases first, lessening the
potential of sanctioning for cases that remain—especially white-color
cases, which require proportionately greater amounts of resources for
successful investigation, prosecution, and sanctioning.

ORGANIZATIONAL ENVIRONMENTS

Recent advances in organizational theory have only begun to be
extensively applied to the sanctioning arm of the criminal justice
system—courts (Mohr, 1976). The growing literature on organizational
environments, in particular (Aldrich and Pfeffer, 1976), needs to be
integrated further into research on criminal justice agencies.
Organization-environment relations are important for assessing what
the specific effects of environmental demands are for the organization in
question and how well it manages its environment. Attempts to
"manage the environment" may include practices which seek to
influence other organizations in that environment. Criminal justice
officials, for example, may try to manage agencies outside their own
control in a "quasi-official" manner, as well as taking care of
organizational matters of their own. Such relations which center on
attempts to control other organizations in the environment may become
more important and necessary as available resources within each agency
decline relative to task requirements, making mutual cooperation and
instruction imperative for continued organizational maintenance.
Police-prosecutor relations provide a clear example of this
phenomenon. As prosecutor caseloads increase, a change may occur in
what constitutes "acceptable input" from police agencies. Under such
conditions of organizational strain, more extensive personal contact
becomes necessary for effective police-prosecutor relations (McIntyre,
1976).

In regard to the more general issue of organization-environment
relations, one recent study provides a promising framework for future
research, especially on courts. Heydebrand (1977) has empirically
examined the relations between environmental demands and the
complexity of task structure in federal district courts. His analysis

indicates that the current fiscal crisis has put increasing pressure on courts to become bureaucratic-administrative rather than simply adjudicative-adversarial institutions. More specifically, Heydebrand documents the "transformation of the judiciary that results from changes in its socioeconomic and political context which generate an increasing demand for judicial services at a time of relative decline in fiscal resources" (1977: 765).

From a political economy perspective, pressures to reduce the expenditures of formal social control mechanisms, given the "fiscal crisis" (O'Connor, 1973; Scull, 1977), have helped highlight the problem of organizational capacity. For example, regarding community release programs, Scull (1977: 152) notes that

> this shift in social control styles and practices must be viewed as dependent upon a reflection of more extensive and deep-seated changes in the social organization of advanced capitalist societies. In particular, it reflects the structural pressures to curtail sharply the costly system of segregative control once welfare payments, providing a subsistence existence for elements of the surplus population, make available a viable alternative to management in an institution. Such structural pressures are greatly intensified by the fiscal crisis encountered in varying degrees at different levels of the state apparatus. . . . It is the pervasiveness and intensity of these pressures, and their mutually reinforcing character, which account for most of the characteristic features of the new system of community "care and treatment."

While Scull directs his argument against the "liberal rhetoric" surrounding the use of release programs for mental patients, his reasoning could extend to criminal justice institutions as well. Both prisons and mental hospitals represent expensive alternatives to probation and community treatment. As government resources decline, pressure to release those confined in *all types* of government institutions should increase. The notion of general deterrence through conventional methods of sanctioning becomes more problematic as such social structural changes take place.

Given a state of declining government resources brought about by fiscal crisis, "it is not surprising . . . that courts have growing difficulty in disposing of their cases, with the result that they accumulate large backlogs and impose long delays" (Heydebrand, 1977: 812). Thus, the extent and nature of various social conflicts which help define the organizational task structures of courts "raise considerable theoretical and empirical doubts about the conceptions of law and state as monolithic and autonomous entities" (p. 814).

As mentioned earlier, Heydebrand's analysis focuses on the relations between the environment and the complexity of task structure in federal district courts. Similar analyses on resource allocations and dispositions in criminal courts, as well as in other criminal justice organizations, can lead to further knowledge in this area. A major point that needs elaboration in such research concerns the limitations to autonomous action by official agencies due to environmental exigencies that produce adaptations not wholly in keeping with espoused organizational goals.

Although the above analyses do not explicitly address the question of environmental demands and criminal justice, the results have important implications for such research, especially concerning the ability of such institutions to control crime.

CONCLUSION

The activities of criminal justice agencies are likely to be affected by many factors that are not evident to lawmakers or the public. In many respects punishment policy is a political phenomenon (Wright, 1973), but the actual functioning of the criminal justice system is less so. A complex network of social and organizational relations among agencies accounts for the manner in which sanctions are generated and administered. Policy proposals that seek crime control through increased sanctioning in one part of the system usually ignore the ramifications of such changes for other elements within the system. Crackdowns by police may result in fewer court filings per arrest and fewer dispositions per filing. Laws that provide for severe mandatory sentences will likely produce changes in offense-charging and plea-bargaining procedures.

Until we recognize that the simple notion that "increased penalties reduce crime" is conditioned by other social and organizational properties, not the least of which is a limited capacity to respond legally, we are destined to continue the application of piecemeal and largely ineffectual "solutions" to the problem of crime control. As far as the future of punishment policy is concerned, the inevitable relationship between punishment and the social structure must be taken into account when considering proposals to reduce crime. That is, we must realize that both the social problems of crime and criminal sanctioning are reflections of larger social, political, and economic conflicts. The failure to do so will lead to little or no progress. Regarding penal policy, the words of Rusche and Kirchheimer (1939: 207) are as true today as they were four decades ago:

> The penal system of any given society is not an isolated phenomenon subject only to its own special laws. It is an integral part of the whole system, and shares its aspirations and its defects. . . . So long as the social consciousness is not in a position to comprehend and act upon the necessary connection between a progressive penal program and progress in general, any project for penal reform can have but doubtful success, and failures will be attributed to the inherent wickedness of human nature rather than to the social system. . . . There is a paradox in the fact that the progress of human knowledge has made the problem of penal treatment more comprehensible and soluble than ever, while the question of a fundamental revision in the policy of punishment seems to be further away today than ever before because of its functional dependence on the given social order.

Simply put, the matter comes to this: First, deterrence and crime control of any significant degree will be achieved only by attending to more fundamental root issues than the structure of legal penalties, issues such as poverty and inequality (Braithwaite, 1979). Second, system capacity—that is, the limited extent of criminal justice personnel and resources—will frustrate attempts to deter crime merely by increasing penalties, even if (and this is arguable) such penalties might be at all effective as deterrents to crime in the first place.

REFERENCES

ALDRICH, H. E. and J. PFEFFER (1976) "Environments of organizations." Annual Rev. of Sociology 2: 79-105.

BALBUS, I. (1973) The Dialectics of Legal Repression. New Brunswick, NJ: Transaction.

BLACK, D. J. (1970) "Production of crime rates." Amer. Soc. Rev. 35: 733-748.

BRAITHWAITE, J. (1979) Crime, Inequality and Social Policy. London: Routledge & Kegan Paul.

CARROLL, J. (1981) "U.S. judge orders transfer of 300 from state prison." Louisville Courier Journal, October 23, B1.

DURKHEIM, E. (1966) The Rules of Sociological Method. New York: Free Press.

EISENSTEIN, J. and H. JACOB (1977) Felony Justice: An Organizational Analysis of Criminal Courts. Boston: Little, Brown.

ERIKSON, K. T. (1966) Wayward Puritans. New York: John Wiley.

FEELEY, M. M. (1975) "The effects of heavy caseloads." Presented at the annual meetings of the American Political Science Association, San Francisco, September 5.

———(1973) "Two models of the criminal justice system: an organizational perspective." Law and Society Rev. 7: 407-425.

GALLIHER, J. F., J. L. McCARTNEY, and B. E. BAUM (1974) "Nebraska's marijuana law: a case of unexpected legislative innovation." Law and Society Rev. 8: 441-455.

GEERKEN, M. and W. R. GOVE (1977) "Deterrence, overload, and incapacitation: an empirical evaluation." Social Forces 56: 424-447.

GIBBS, J. P. (1978) "Another rush to judgment on the deterrence question." Criminology 16: 22-30.

HENSHEL, R. L. (1978) "Considerations on the deterrence and system capacity models." Criminology 16: 35-46.

HEUMANN, M. (1978) Plea Bargaining: The Experiences of Prosecutors, Judges and Defense Attorneys. Chicago: Univ. of Chicago Press.

———(1975) "A note on plea bargaining and case pressure." Law and Society Rev. 9: 515-528.

HEYDEBRAND, W. V. (1977) "The context of public bureaucracies: an organizational analysis of federal district courts." Law and Society Rev. 11: 759-822.

JACOB, H. and M. J. RICH (1981) "The effects of police on crime: a second look." Law and Society Rev. 15: 109-122.

KATZ, J. (1980) "The social movement against white-collar crime," pp. 161-184 in E. Bittner and S. L. Messinger (eds.) Criminology Review Yearbook. Beverly Hills, CA: Sage.

McINTYRE, D. M. (1976) "Impediments to effective police-prosecutor relationships." Amer. Criminal Law Rev. 13: 201-231.

MOHR, L. B. (1976) "Organizations, decisions, and courts." Law and Society Rev. 10: 621-642.

NAGIN, D. (1978) "Crime rates, sanction levels, and constraints on prison population." Law and Society Rev. 12: 341-366.

NARDULLI, P. F. (1979) "The caseload controversy and the study of criminal courts." J. of Criminal Law and Criminology 70: 89-101.

O'CONNOR, J. (1973) The Fiscal Crisis of the State. New York: St. Martin's.

PEPINSKY, H. E. (1980) Crime Control Strategies: An Introduction to the Study of Crime. New York: Oxford Univ. Press.

PONTELL, H. N. (1979) "Deterrence and system capacity: crime and punishment in California." Ph.D. dissertation, State University of New York at Stony Brook.

———(1978) "Deterrence: theory versus practice." Criminology 16: 3-22.

POUND, R. (1975) Criminal Justice in America. New York: Plenum.

REISS, A. J. (1971) The Police and the Public. New Haven: Yale Univ. Press.

RUSCHE, G. and O. KIRCHHEIMER (1939) Punishment and Social Structure. New York: Columbia Univ. Press.

SCULL, A. T. (1977) Decarceration. Englewood-Cliffs, NJ: Prentice-Hall.

TITTLE, C. R. (1978) "Comment on 'Deterrence: theory versus practice.'" Criminology 16: 31-34.

TOBY, J. (1981) "Deterrence without punishment." Criminology 19: 195-209.

WRIGHT, E. (1973) The Politics of Punishment: A Critical Analysis of Prisons in America. New York: Harper & Row.

David O. Friedrichs
University of Scranton

9

WEBERIAN CONCEPTIONS OF RATIONALITY AND LEGITIMACY
Transcending Parochialism in Criminological Theory

The claim has been made that the three great "masters" of contemporary sociological theory are Durkheim, Marx, and Weber (see Sherman, 1974). In the 1950s and 1960s the influence of Durkheim was most evident. Robert Merton's celebrated essay "Social Structure and Anomie," originally published in 1938 (Merton, 1968), utilized a modified version of a Durkheimian concept, anomie, and inspired a whole generation of criminological theorists (for example, see Clinard, 1964). The structural-functionalism and consensus model so conspicuous—if not entirely dominant—during this period drew heavily on an interpretation of Durkheim's work. While it has been shown that Durkheim regarded societal stability as problematic (see Hunt, 1982), he also advanced a perspective and set of concepts consistent with a statist orientation toward crime and criminality.

AUTHOR'S NOTE: This chapter is partially derived from two very different papers, one originally presented at the Fourth Annual Max Weber Colloquium, William Paterson College of New Jersey, October 30-31, 1980, and the other originally presented at the 33rd Annual Meetings of the American Society of Criminology, Washington, D.C., November 1981. It has benefited greatly from a thorough critique of an earlier draft by Hal Pepinsky; as I have somewhat perversely chosen not to follow all his suggestions, he shouldn't be blamed for the remaining shortcomings. Preparation of the chapter was aided by a University of Scranton Faculty Research Grant.

In the 1970s, Marx began to emerge as an important source of theoretical inspiration, most particularly—in the American context—in the work of Richard Quinney and William Chambliss (see Friedrichs, 1980b). Beginning with a reaffirmation of the tenets of conflict theory, some sociologists during this period subjected the consensus perspective—especially in its structural-functionalist form—to vigorous challenge (see Gouldner, 1970). Marx's conceptions of a capitalist system, and of class struggle, were adopted as basic points of departure for a criminological perspective variously described as new, Marxist, critical, or radical. The main parameters of this perspective, and the various challenges to it, are readily accessible (e.g., see Beirne and Quinney, 1982; Greenberg, 1981; Inciardi, 1980). For present purposes we can simply note that over the past decade or so the Marxist influence in criminology has been firmly established; it remains highly controversial, and its future direction is not entirely clear.[1]

What of the third great master, Max Weber? Does his work provide any basis for the advancement of criminological theory, as it evolves through the 1980s? To date Weber has had little influence on the field of criminology.[2] On the whole only marginal citations of Weber can be found in criminology textbooks, usually in the form of a cursory reference to some concept such as "the protestant ethic," "bureaucracy," or "status groups."[3] Weber's "value-free" posture has been influential, albeit often indirectly and certainly in a misunderstood way. Of course, Weber's presence is most pronounced in the sociology of law (e.g., Grace and Wilkinson, 1978; Cain, 1980; Beirne, 1982). Law and legal institutions were in fact recognized by all three sociological masters to be important elements in understanding broader social phenomena. Sykes has observed that "although Karl Marx, Max Weber, and Emile Durkheim had an interest in legal institutions, later theorists in the social sciences seemed reluctant to follow their lead" (1978: 33). Sykes is surely correct in suggesting an emerging reconciliation between criminology and the study of criminal law, or the sociology of law (1978: 35-36). The sociology of law itself has only recently been characterized by a serious reemergence of theoretical explanations (see Hunt, 1981: 47). Insofar as these trends persist, the potential for a Weberian influence in criminology becomes that much greater.

In one of the most substantial attempts to develop a sociology of criminal law, Chambliss and Seidman (1971) draw quite considerably on Weber's work, with special attention to his conceptions of state power, bureaucracy, rationality, and legitimacy. Their application of these concepts is selective and limited, however, and in at least some cases—for example, regarding legitimacy (1971: 350-356)—open to challenge.

Some of the work of Austin Turk (e.g., 1977), the leading exponent of nonpartisan conflict theory in the sociology of criminal law, is described as presenting a "Weberian version of conflict theory".[4] Turk himself has not drawn directly on Weber in all his recent work, but others have adopted his conception of "Weberian criminology" (see Chan, 1981; Huff, 1980).[5] At least one attempt has been made—inspired by Turk's lead—to apply a Weberian criminology to an understanding of conflict and control in a developing country (see Morden, 1980).

Other works published in the 1970s that could be classified as contributions to the sociology of criminal law have also drawn at least selectively on Weber's ideas. Pepinsky (1976) has considered responses to criminal law in two very different types of society, the United States and the People's Republic of China; he utilizes conceptions central to Weber's work—legal rationality and formalism—as elements in his analysis. Balbus (1977) also incorporates Weberian conceptions into his study of criminal justice system responses to urban riots. He finds, for example, that repression by formal rationality is beset by contradictions but ultimately involves an effective response to the short-term need to maintain order and the long-term need to maintain legitimacy (1977: 257).

The scholars just mentioned have demonstrated the relevance of Weber's contributions for extending the horizons of criminological theory. Recent work in the rapidly growing area of interest centering on white-collar and corporate crime cites Weber selectively (e.g., see Geis and Stotland, 1980); we can also find utilizations of Weberian concepts in the study of specific justice system processes, such as appellate decision making (e.g., see Lanza-Kaduce, 1981). Such initiatives are still very much the exception, however; they are at least suggestive of a potential for further development. In some respects Weber's work, relative to Marx's and Durkheim's, is the most complex and least amenable to simplified formulations, which may help explain the limited nature of his influence in criminology. We can, however, draw on his ideas without necessarily adopting any existing notion of a Weberian criminology. The present status of our understanding of two central Weberian conceptions—rationality and legitimacy—would seem worthy of discussion, with a consideration of further possible applications relevant to the development of criminological theory.[6]

THE CONCEPT OF RATIONALITY

A major theme of Weber's work—perhaps *the* major theme—utilizes a conception of rationality as the pivotal motif of modern social development. For Weber the emergence of Western capitalism and an orientation toward rationality were intimately linked, with a complex of reciprocal effects (see Weber, 1968). While rationality was not exclusively a product of contemporary Western society, it was in fact an increasingly conspicuous dimension of contemporary life. It has been suggested that Weber regarded rationality as something that both contributes to and curtails freedom in the modern environment (see Levine, 1981). The concept of rationality and rationalization is referred to in many places in Weber's voluminous work; his premature death prevented the revision and completion of his major work, and Levine notes that Weber's concept of rationality was "multiply ambiguous" in that he did not produce a promised conceptual exposition of its many possible meanings (1981: 10). One recent commentator (Kalberg, 1980) identifies four types of rationality in Weber's work: practical, theoretical, substantive, and formal. Another commentator (Eisen, 1978) identifies six interdependent, albeit essentially consistent elements in Weber's use of the term rationality: purpose, calculability, control, logical, universality, and systematic.[7] All of these students of Weber's work, while critical in various ways of his conception of rationalization, concede its basic value as a point of departure for the interpretation of diverse social phenomena. Weber himself probably intended his types of rationality to serve essentially as "heuristic tools" to be applied to the analysis of sociocultural processes (see Kalberg, 1980: 1172). In a general way Weber compels us, through his discussion of rationality, to attend to the complex of implications of this type of orientation.

Criminology and criminological theory can benefit from more systematic attention to Weber's analysis of rationality on several different levels. On the macrotheoretical level we are provided with a key concept which contributes to our understanding of the larger social and political context within which law develops and crime occurs. The specific identification of dimensions of rationality—or their absence—provides an important basis for cross-cultural comparative analysis regarding law and crime. Within the context of contemporary Western capitalist nations rationality can be applied to the study of basic legal processes and institutions.[8] Finally, rationality is a concept which must be incorporated into any theoretical or empirical interpretation of compliance with legal order.[9] In this sense Weber's writings on rationality can advance the emerging project in criminological theory of reconciling the sociology of law with traditional etiological concerns.

THE CONCEPT OF LEGITIMACY

Weber's discussion of legitimacy and legitimation constitutes a basic contribution to the social science literature; he deals with it in various places in his work (see Weber, 1954, 1964, 1968). Bensman (1979) is generally correct, I believe, in asserting that Weber did not construct a full-fledged theory of legitimacy, and he utilized the concept itself in a multitude of ways. The five different meanings identified by Bensman (1979) include notions of belief, claim, justification, promise, and self-justification. For present purposes we may contend that legitimacy is broadly construed in Weberian terms as that which is justified ("right") and demanding of support ("binding"). "Power" will attempt to cultivate a belief in its legitimacy; the stability of an order or system is related to the level of legitimacy it is capable of generating. The task of the sociologist is not to evaluate the legitimacy of an order as such, but rather to identify the nature of responses to that order. Weber, in a significant passage, observed: "Naturally the legitimacy of a system of authority may be treated sociologically only as the probability that to a relevant degree the appropriate attitudes will exist, and the corresponding practical conduct ensue" (1964: 326). An individual may be oriented toward coexisting—even contradictory—orders, and conduct may be oriented simultaneously toward different orders. Compliance with a legal order as such should not be confused with legitimation; some degree of legitimation is required for the very emergence of, or continued endurance of, the legal order. Acquiescence is usually a combination of self-interest, tradition, and belief in legality; the sociologist's task is to determine which type of validity is the typical one.

It is not possible here to undertake an examination of the numerous interpretive problems raised by Weber's treatment of legitimacy; I have undertaken such a preliminary examination elsewhere (see Friedrichs, 1980c). For present purposes it can be noted that there has been an extensive debate on the role of ethical and natural law elements in Weber's legitimacy conceptualization, on the hypothetically paradoxical variations between Weber's different "listings" of types of action, legitimation, and domination (or legitimate authority), and on the *relative* importance of legitimacy as an element of a stable social order.[10]

Following at least one understanding of Weber, it can be suggested that in the final analysis legitimacy is meaningful, mainly in terms of ascriptions and orientations rather than in terms of claims, although from a sociological perspective legitimacy is measurable only in terms of actual manifestations and consequences. Legitimation of an order implies acceptance at a minimum, but need not necessarily mean absolute commitment. In contemporary society legal-rational grounds for legitimation have achieved increasing significance, but Weber also recognized the actual or potential effects of value-based appeals transcending such limitations. An order is guaranteed relative to its ability to generate a certain level of support, but in contemporary society such support may not be unanimous, or even represented by a numerical majority.

If Weber's work on legitimacy is to contribute substantially to the advancement of criminological theory, a number of tasks must be undertaken. First, the concept of legitimacy must be fully explored and its various dimensions articulated. This effort begins with a thorough analysis of Weber's own conception; it must then consider the formidable literature on the concept that has appeared since Weber's time (as well as before and during his time) and must aspire to the formulation of an integrated, definitive conception of legitimacy and legitimation. Especially relevant for the concerns of criminology are the dual dimensions of the sense of obligation to comply and the explicit or implicit generation of expectations by the legal order.

An understanding of legitimacy allows us to approach the significant issue of a legitimacy "crisis." Elsewhere I have advanced a conceptual analysis of the legitimacy crisis in the United States in terms of attitudinal, behavioral, and structural dimensions (see Friedrichs, 1980a) and have also explored in a preliminary way some of the consequences of the crisis for the legal order (Friedrichs, 1979) and the criminal justice system (Friedrichs, 1981a). For present purposes one can simply claim that developments pertaining to crime and legal order should be understood in terms of the context of an evolving legitimacy crisis. Such an understanding provides one approach for relating these developments to international events and domestic politics.

The existence of widely diffused involvement in illegal activity by those who profit most directly from the perpetuation of the existing order—white-collar professionals, corporate executives, and government officials—deserves to be examined in the light of the legitimacy issue.[11] Conventional ghetto or "street" crime raises the question of the extent to which widely diffused involvement in illegal activity can be specifically understood in terms of delegitimation. The general increase in violent crime in our society over the past two decades has varied inversely (up to a point) with the decline of confidence in the leadership and faith in major institutions; the links between both perceptions and manifestations of violence and the evolving varieties of legitimation must be more fully explored (see Friedrichs, 1981b). In the realm of victimless crime, shifting policies, attitudes and behavioral patterns pertinent to this type of activity can be interpreted within the context of legitimacy crisis; an understanding of the problem of legitimacy suggests the extraordinary difficulties of advancing satisfactory and effective policy responses in this area (see Friedrichs, 1980d).

The concept of legitimacy—with critical roots in Weber's formulations—can serve as a key element in the development of a criminological theory. It has a special potential for advancing our understanding of the complex reciprocal relationship between the legal realm and patterns of noncompliant activity.

TRANSCENDING PAROCHIALISM: WEBER AND BEYOND

The status of law and legal order in America today is in flux. We find references to diminished confidence in law (Vago, 1981: 20), calls for more informal justice (Abel, 1981), and theoretical projections of the demise of law (Turk, 1979). Although the specific nature and dimensions of the crisis in the legal realm is open to variable interpretation, two premises have informed this chapter: (1) A crisis on some level is indeed real, with multiple effects on crime and criminal justice; and (2) Weber's conceptions of "rationality" and "legitimacy" can serve as significant points of departure for a deeper understanding of this crisis and its ramifications. In an increasingly rationalized society, legitimation of law and the legal system becomes increasingly problematic.

The continually evolving character of sociological theory is reflected in the interrelated subdisciplinary areas of criminology and the sociology of law. To date the tendency has been to contrast the Durkheimian (functionalist) and Marxist (conflict) heritage;

Chambliss's (1976) effort in this regard has been widely cited. Hunt (1981: 72-72) recently observed that none of the existing theoretical positions has fully resolved the problem of opposing (consensual and conflictual) characteristics of the law, and the call for drawing on both Durkheim and Marx has been issued (e.g., see Inverarity, 1980). Most criminologists identified with a Marxist tradition would probably reject that call, and at least some have been specifically antagonistic to Weber.[12] On the other hand, a growing number of scholars seem to acknowledge the importance of both Marx and Weber for advancing our understanding of contemporary law-related phenomena.[13] It was said of Weber himself that he was engaged in a lifelong debate with the "ghost" of Karl Marx (see Wrong, 1970: 52); a challenge for the serious radical criminologist dedicated to the development of a viable and convincing theoretical framework is to address this debate and consider possible areas of resolution.[14] To adopt the work of either Marx or Weber (in both cases incomplete and fragmentary in certain respects) as a comprehensive guide to contemporary social reality is dogmatic and simpleminded; it is surely possible to embrace a generalized radical framework and still profit from the conceptual leads and qualifying principles advanced by Weber.

The potential for criminology to transcend its traditional parochialism has been amply demonstrated over the past decade. The integration of criminology and the sociology of criminal law is basic to this endeavor. A profound understanding of crime and legal order is ultimately openminded; it attends to anomie, to a capitalist economy, and to legitimacy in relation to rationalization. Crime and legal order in contemporary American society must be interpreted in terms of its mass character, the contradictions inherent in its democratic ideals, and the problematic influence of its Judeo-Christian heritage, in addition to the central role of a capitalist economy. The recent efforts to recover the history of crime and criminal justice (e.g., Brewer and Styles, 1980; Inciardi and Faupel, 1980) are critically important. In an ever-shrinking world a comparative criminology becomes essential (e.g., see Shelley, 1981). And an emerging world-system perspective (see Wallerstein, 1980; Chase-Dunn, 1980; and Camilleri, 1981) suggests we might consider law and crime within the context of a particular nation-state's location in the world capitalist economy.[15]

A truly potent, sophisticated criminological theory is one which is unified with a broader theory of social order and human action.[16] The complex interaction between law and the structure of the legal order on the one hand and those forms of behavior and action designated "criminal" on the other must ultimately be understood within a sophisticated transdisciplinary framework. Max Weber—described by Dennis Wrong as "the last universal genius of the social sciences" (1970: 1)—represents one important source of inspiration and insight for those who would transcend parochialism in criminological theory.

NOTES

1. See Friedrichs (1980b) and Michalowski (1981) for some speculation on the future direction of this paradigm.

2. Huff asserts that "Weber's writings on social organization are regarded as classics and are extensively utilized by contemporary criminologists in the analysis of criminal justice agencies. Weber's legacy in criminology . . . is indeed profound" (1980: 73). Weber's interpretation of bureaucracy has been at least indirectly influential, but Huff's assertion is not really documented—discussion of Turk's adoption of Weberian conflict theory aside—and can, I believe, be challenged in terms of its more general implications.

3. Among recent criminology textbook authors, Daniel Glaser (1978) seems to cite Weber most frequently. See Friedrichs (1980c) for a general review of textbook citations.

4. Turk submits, in one piece:

For Weberians, criminality is coming to be seen as a category defined solely by the actions of the authorities of *any* politically organized society. . . . Criminality is a political concept. . . . Weberians use a 'relativistic amorality' in defining criminality as whatever is made punishable by the actions of whoever exercises the power of the state [1977: 217].

5. Huff, in discussing this perspective, makes the useful point that it is more applicable to explaining criminal activity in socialist societies than is a Marxist perspective (1980: 73); the inadequacy of the latter perspective in this regard has been one of the most enduring criticisms directed at radical criminology.

6. Given the limitations of space, many other relevant areas of Weber's work—such as his methodology and his conceptions of law, bureaucracy, and stratification—will not be directly attended to here.

7. Eisen also claims that Weber's distinction between formal and substantive rationality is theoretically confusing and substantially biased (1978). He argues: "Formal rationality is not merely formal, but substantive: it has 'real' implications. Substantive rationality is often merely formal: it lacks 'real' repercussions; i.e., power" (Eisen, 1978: 66).

8. Glaser (1981: 4) recently predicted: "Criminologists will monitor all aspects of the criminal justice system as it manifests what Max Weber foresaw as an increasing search for rationality, for guidance by logical rules and objective data, which pervades all types of organizations." See Lanza-Kaduce (1981) for one attempt to utilize Weberian concepts to interpret criminal justice system processes (in this case, appellate decision making).

9. Cain has made the important point that "rationality plays a part in theories of both structure (e.g., bureaucracy) and subjective state (e.g., orientations to orders) and thus yields 'obvious' links between the two" (1980: 81).

10. For recent critiques of Weber's conception of legitimacy see Grafstein (1981) and Merquior (1979). Grafstein takes Weber's use of the concept to task for its alleged failure to signify a normative evaluation of a political regime (effectively, its imputation of beliefs which in turn accounts for the stability of regimes). Merquior claims that "Weber did not pay attention to illegitimacy because he defined his types of legitimacy *from the viewpoint of the rulers,* not of the ruled" (1979: 132).

11. There are also indications that increasing exposure of "elite deviance" contributes to the generation of a crisis of confidence (Simon and Eitzen, 1982: vii-viii, 1-6) or legitimacy crisis (Friedrichs, 1980a: 549-550). Simon and Eitzen posit the following, I believe correctly:

> The crisis of confidence in the United States has caught most social scientists by surprise. We lack a well-integrated body of theory and research that adequately explains the causes and predicts the consequences of the elite immorality and economic crises of our times [1982: vii].

12. For example, Walton accuses Weber of accepting "the inevitability of (a) domination, (b) permanent injustice in law and (c) the supposed independent nature of law" (1976: 8).

13. I have in mind British(born) students of the sociology of law, including Alan Hunt, Maureen Cain, and Piers Beirne.

14. Balbus (1977) and Pepinsky (1976), cited earlier, represent two efforts to draw on both Marx and Weber. For recent comments on the relationship between Weber's work and at least one Marxist tradition in scholarship, see Castelnuovo (1979) and Greisman and Ritzer (1981).

15. See Greenberg (1980) and Friedrichs (forthcoming) for some preliminary discussion of the relationship between such macro-level theoretical perspectives and our understanding of law, or legitimacy. For one recent critique of the world-system perspective see Howe and Sica (1980).

16. This chapter focuses especially on macro-level theory. An earlier draft at least tentatively explored hypothetical directions for micro-level theory; reference was made here to moral developmental psychology and existential philosophy as schools of thought providing at least a potential for further application in criminology. For reasons of space this discussion has been omitted here.

REFERENCES

ABEL, R. L. (1981) "Conservative conflict and the reproduction of capitalism: the role of informal justice." Int. J. of the Sociology of Law 9: 245-267.

BALBUS, I. (1977) The Dialectics of Legal Repression. New Brunswick, NJ: Transaction.

BEIRNE, P. (1982) "Ideology and rationality in Max Weber's sociology of law," pp. 44-62 in P. Beirne and R. Quinney (eds.) Marxism and Law. New York: John Wiley.

——— and R. QUINNEY (1982) Marxism and Law. New York: John Wiley.

BENSMAN, J. (1979) "Max Weber's concept of legitimacy: an evaluation," pp. 17-48 in A. J. Vidich and R. M. Glassman (eds.) Conflict and Control. Beverly Hills, CA: Sage.

BREWER, J. and J. STYLES [eds.] (1980) An Ungovernable People: The English and Their Law in the Seventeenth and Eighteenth Centuries. New Brunswick, NJ: Rutgers Univ. Press.

CAIN, M. (1980) "The limits of idealism: Max Weber and the sociology of law," pp. 53-83 in S. Spitzer (ed.) Research in Law and Sociology, Vol. III. Greenwich, CT: JAI Press.

CAMILLERI, J. (1981) "The advanced capitalist state and the contemporary world crisis." Science and Society 45: 130-158.

CASTELNUOVO, S. (1979) "Public interest law: crisis of legitimacy or quest for legal order autonomy," pp. 231- 249 in S. Spitzer (ed.) Research in Law and Sociology, Vol. II. Greenwich, CT: JAI Press.

CHAMBLISS, W. J. (1976) "Functional and conflict theories of crime: the heritage of Emile Durkheim and Karl Marx," pp. 1-28 in W. J. Chambliss and M. Mankoff (eds.) Whose Law? What Order? A Conflict Approach to Criminology. New York: John Wiley.

———and R. B. SEIDMAN (1971) Law, Order and Power. Reading, MA: Addison-Wesley.

CHAN, J.B.L. (1981) "From Hobbes to Marx: a study of man, society and criminality in classical to contemporary theories." Canadian Criminology Forum (Spring): 118-128.

CHASE-DUNN, C. K. (1980) "Socialist states in the capitalist world economy," Social Problems 27: 505-525.

CLINARD, M. [ed.] (1964) Anomie and Deviant Behavior. New York: Free Press.

EISEN, A. (1978) "The meanings and confusions of Weberian 'rationality.' " British J. of Sociology 29: 57-69.

FRIEDRICHS, D. O. (1981a) "Criminal justice and the crisis of confidence." Justice Reporter 1: 1-6.

——— (1981b) "Violence and the politics of crime." Social Research 48: 135-156.

——— (1980a) "The legitimacy crisis in the United States: a conceptual analysis." Social Problems 27: 540-555.

——— (1980b) "Radical criminology in the U.S.: an interpretive understanding," pp. 35-60 in J. A. Inciardi (ed.) Radical Criminology: The Coming Crises. Beverly Hills, CA: Sage.

——— (1980c) "Weber's conception of legitimation and the theory of criminal justice." Presented at the Fourth Annual Max Weber Colloquium at the William Paterson College of New Jersey, October.

——— (1980d) "Victimless crime and the problem of legitimacy." Presented at the annual meeting of the Academy of Criminal Justice Sciences, Oklahoma City, March.

——— (1979) "Law and the legitimacy crisis," pp. 290-311 in R. G. Iacovetta and D. H. Chang (eds.) Critical Issues in Criminal Justice. Durham, NC: Carolina Academic Press.

——— (forthcoming) "The political economy of the world system and the legitimacy crisis." Int. J. of Critical Sociology.

GEIS, G. and E. STOTLAND [eds.] (1980) White-Collar Crime: Theory and Research. Beverly Hills, CA: Sage.

GIBBONS, D. C. (1979) The Criminological Enterprise: Theories and Perspectives. Englewood Cliffs, NJ: Prentice-Hall.

GLASER, D. (1981) "Theoretical and empirical concerns of criminologists in the 1980s." Criminal News. ASA Criminology Section (Winter): 3-5.

——— (1978) Crime in Our Changing Society. New York: Holt, Rinehart & Winston.

GOULDNER, A. W. (1970) The Coming Crisis in Western Sociology. New York: Basic Books.

GRACE, C. and P. WILKINSON (1978) Sociological Inquiry and Legal Phenomena. New York: St. Martin's.

GRAFSTEIN, R. (1981) "The failure of Weber's conception of legitimacy: its causes and implications." J. of Politics 43: 456-472.

GREENBERG, D. (1981) Crime and Capitalism: Readings in Marxist Criminology. Palo Alto, CA: Mayfield.

——— (1980) "Law and development in light of dependency theory," pp. 129-159 in S. Spitzer (ed.) Research in Law and Sociology, Vol. III. Greenwich, CT: JAI Press.

GREISMAN, H. C. and G. RITZER (1981) "Max Weber, critical theory and the administered world." Qualitative Sociology 4: 34-55.

HOWE, G. and A. M. SICA (1980) "Political economy, imperialism and the problem of world system theory," pp. 235-286 in S. G. McNall and G. N. Howe (eds.) Current Perspectives in Social Theory. Greenwich, CT: JAI Press.

HUFF, C. R. (1980) "Conflict theory in criminology," pp. 61-77 in J. A. Inciardi (ed.) Radical Criminology: The Coming Crises. Beverly Hills, CA: Sage.

HUNT, A. (1982) "Emile Durkheim: towards a sociology of law," pp. 27-43 in P. Beirne and R. Quinney (eds.) Marxism and Law. New York: John Wiley.

——— (1981) "Dichotomy and contradiction in the sociology of law." British J. of Law & Society 8: 47-77.

INCIARDI, J. A. [ed.] (1980) Radical Criminology: The Coming Crises. Beverly Hills, CA: Sage.

INVERARITY, J. (1980) "Theories of the political creation of deviance—legacies of conflict theory, Marx and Durkheim," pp. 175-217 in P. Lauderdale (ed.) A Political Analysis of Deviance. Minneapolis: Univ. of Minnesota Press.

KALBERG, S. (1980) "Max Weber's types of rationality: cornerstones for the analysis of rationalization processes in history." Amer. J. of Sociology 85: 1145-1179.

LANZA-KADUCE, L. (1981) "Formality, neutrality, and goal-rationality: the legacy of Weber in legal thought." Presented at the 33rd Annual Meetings of the American Society of Criminology, Washington, D.C., November.

LEVINE, D. N. (1981) "Rationality and freedom: Weber and beyond." Soc. Inquiry 51: 5-26.

MERQUIOR, J. G. (1980) Rousseau and Weber—Two Studies in the Theory of Legitimacy. London: Routledge & Kegan Paul.

MERTON, R. K. (1968) "Social structure and anomie," pp. 185-215 in Social Theory and Social Structure. New York: Free Press.

MICHALOWSKI, R. J. (1981) "Conflict, radical and critical approaches to criminology," pp. 39-52 in I. L. Barak-Glantz and C. R. Huff (eds.) The Mad, the Bad and the Different. Lexington, MA: D. C. Heath.

MORDEN, P. (1980) "Toward a Weberian criminology for developing countries: conflict and control in Malaysia." Canadian Criminology Forum 2: 35-46.

PEPINSKY, H. E. (1976) Crime and Conflict: A Study of Law and Society. New York: Academic.

SHELLEY, L. I. (1981) Crime and Modernization—The Impact of Industrialization and Urbanization on Crime. Carbondale: Southern Illinois Univ. Press.

SHERMAN, L. W. (1974) "Uses of the masters." Amer. Sociologist 9: 176-181.

SIMON, D. R. and D. S. EITZEN (1982) Elite Deviance. Boston: Allyn & Bacon.

SYKES, G. M. (1978) Criminology. New York: Harcourt Brace Jovanovich.

TURK, A. T. (1979) "Conceptions of the demise of law," pp. 12-26 in P. J. Brantingham and J. M. Kress (eds.) Structure, Law and Power. Beverly Hills, CA: Sage.

——— (1977) "Class, conflict, and criminalization." Soc. Focus 10: 209-220.

VAGO, S. (1981) Law and Society. Englewood Cliffs, NJ: Prentice-Hall.

WALLERSTEIN, I. (1980) " 'The withering away of the states.' " Int. J. of the Sociology of Law 8: 369-378.

WEBER, M. (1968) Economy and Society (3 volumes). (G. Roth and C. Wittich, eds.). New York: Bedminster Press.

——— (1964) The Theory of Social and Economic Organization (A. M. Henderson and T. L. Parsons, trans.). New York: Free Press.

——— (1954) On Law in Economy and Society (M. Rheinstein, ed.). Cambridge: Harvard Univ. Press.

WRONG, D. [ed.] (1970) Max Weber. Englewood Cliffs, NJ: Prentice-Hill.

end of chapter 9.32

ABOUT THE AUTHORS

ARNOLD ANDERSON-SHERMAN is Assistant Professor of Sociology at George Mason University. He is currently working on *Sociology: Analysis and Applications*, (with Joseph A. Scimecca), West Publishing Co., (Forthcoming); and *The Social Bases of Politics*, (with Aliza Kolker), Wadsworth Publishing Co., (Forthcoming).

ROBERT M. BOHM is Assistant Professor of Criminal Justice at Jacksonville State University, Jacksonville, Alabama. His major research interest is in the area of criminological theory. Related articles include "Reflexivity and Critical Criminology" in Gary F. Jensen's *Sociology of Delinquency: Current Issues* (Sage, 1981) and "Radical Criminology: An Explication" in *Criminology* (February 1982).

JOHN BRAITHWAITE is Senior Researcher at the Australian Institute of Criminology, Canberra. He is among the more prolific authors in criminology today, having published a number of books, articles, and chapters on white-collar/organizational crime and on class discrimination in criminal justice. Among his works are *Crime, Inequality and Social Policy* (Routledge & Kegan Paul, 1979) and *Corporate Crime in the Pharmaceutical Industry* (Routledge & Kegan Paul, 1982).

NORMAN K. DENZIN, Professor of Sociology at the University of Illinois, Urbana, received his Ph.D. in sociology from the University of Iowa in 1966. He is the author of *The Research Act* (1978) and *Childhood Socialization* (1977) and editor of *Studies in Symbolic Interaction: An Annual Compilation of Research* (JAI Press).

DAVID O. FRIEDRICHS is Assistant Professor of Sociology and Criminal Justice at the University of Scranton. His primary research interests include legitimacy problems of the legal order and radical theory in criminology. Journals publishing his recent articles include *Social Problems, The Justice Reporter, Social Research,* and *Qualitative Sociology.* He contributed two articles to J. A. Inciardi's *Radical Criminology: The Coming Crises* (Sage, 1980). He is Vice President (Elect) of the Association for Humanist Sociology and Chair of the Academy of Criminal Justice Sciences' History of the Field Committee.

JOSEPH HARRISON has been involved in criminological research projects in the United States and in Israel for the last ten years. He has taught university courses in the fields of criminology, sociology, and political science for the State University of New York and for Florida State University. He received his B.A. degree in sociology from SUNY Empire State College (1976); his M.S. in criminology from Florida State University (1978); and his J. D. degree from Vanderbilt University School of Law (1982). In addition to continuing interests in psychopharmacology, Joseph Harrison has published and lectured widely on the issues raised by white-collar crime and governmental criminality. He is currently engaged in research work in Nashville, Tennessee.

DENNIS LONGMIRE is Assistant Professor in the Sociology Department at The Ohio State University, where his current research interests include the examination of ethical issues confronting criminological researchers, violence in penal institutions, the study of alternative styles of justice, and moral/legal sociolization. He received his Ph.D. in criminal justice/criminology from the University of Maryland's Institute of Criminal Justice and Criminology in 1979 and has published several articles in professional journals focusing on various aspects of criminology.

HAROLD E. PEPINSKY is Associate Professor of Forensic Studies and of East Asian Languages and Cultures at Indiana University, Bloomington. He is author of *Crime Control Strategies* (Oxford, 1980) and *Crime and Conflict* (Academic, 1976).

HENRY N. PONTELL is currently Assistant Professor of Social Ecology and Social Science at the University of California, Irvine. He received his Ph.D. in sociology from SUNY at Stony Brook in 1979. He also served as a research associate in the Department of Community and Preventative Medicine, School of Medicine, SUNY at Stony Brook. Professor Pontell has published in the fields of criminology and medical sociology. Besides crime, punishment, and deterrence, his current research interests include white-collar crime, social deviance, and inequality and criminal justice.